EXERCISING
INFLUENCE

EXERCISING INFLUENCE

Third Edition

—— A **GUIDE** FOR ——
MAKING THINGS HAPPEN
at Work, at Home, and in Your Community

B. KIM BARNES

WILEY

Published by John Wiley & Sons, Inc., Hoboken, New Jersey
Published simultaneously in Canada

For general information about our other products and services, please contact our Customer Care Department within the United States at (800) 762-2974, outside the United States at (317) 572-3993 or fax (317) 572-4002.

Wiley publishes in a variety of print and electronic formats and by print-on-demand. Some material included with standard print versions of this book may not be included in e-books or in print-on-demand. If this book refers to media such as a CD or DVD that is not included in the version you purchased, you may download this material at http://booksupport.wiley.com. For more information about Wiley products, visit www.wiley.com.

Library of Congress Cataloging-in-Publication Data is Available:

ISBN 978-1-119-07158-7 (paperback)
ISBN 978-1-119-07170-9 (ePDF)
ISBN 978-1-119-07149-5 (ePub)

Cover Design: Wiley
Cover Illustration courtesy of B. Kim Barnes

Printed in the United States of America

V10014319_092719

This book is dedicated to Abigail, Elizabeth, Emily, and Isaac
—the next generation of influencers.

CONTENTS

ABOUT THIS BOOK

Why Is This Topic Important?

Influencing is something everyone needs to be able to do, but it requires a set of skills and understandings that is rarely taught explicitly. Since 1994, when we introduced our "influence fitness" program, *Exercising Influence: Building Relationships and Getting Results*, participants have asked for a book that they can read for further development. This book, as its name implies, is intended to be a practical guide to developing effective influencing skills independent of the seminar.

What Can You Achieve with This Book?

The book provides a means for reflecting on your current approach to influencing others, as well as examples, insights, tools, and skill practice opportunities that will help you to become a more effective influencer. You will develop a greater appreciation for the many opportunities you have daily to make your life and work more satisfying and meaningful through influential communication. You can use this book in several ways:

- As a general information book, to be read in its entirety.
- As a resource for specific ideas about various aspects of influencing. If you use it in this way, you may want to read the first part and then use the rest for reference, as appropriate.
- As a guide to a structured influence fitness program that can be implemented alone or with others in a conscious and sequential way for the purpose of developing and improving skills.
- As a follow-up to or preparation for attending the course, *Exercising Influence: Building Relationships and Getting Results*™. For information on this course, see the first item in the Resources section.

How Is the Book Organized?

The material in this book is divided into three parts. The first part, Exercising Influence, focuses on developing the skills and understanding required to be an effective influencer. The second part, Planning for Influence, provides practical advice on preparing for, implementing, and reviewing an actual influence opportunity. The third part, Special Issues in Influence, explores important issues that arise in the process of exercising your influence, as well as special applications of influence skills. Each of the short chapters within the sections covers an area that is relevant to influencing in all aspects of life. The remainder of the book includes appendixes with supplementary material.

In this book, I have used several metaphors that offer parallels to this complex topic. Developing influence skills is like fitness training, the planning process is like preparing for a safari, and the actual experience of influencing is like improvisational theater. The process of becoming an effective influencer is a lifelong journey. To help guide us on this journey, I have selected some quotations from Ralph Waldo Emerson, whose wisdom and good sense speak to us across 180 years. Emerson's essays, most of them written in the 1830s and 1840s, are especially full of relevant observations and advice of value to those of us interested in building relationships and getting results through influence. In an 1844 essay, Emerson wrote, "This is that which we call character—a reserved force which acts directly by presence, and without means." That is as good a definition of the power of influence as we are likely to find.

ACKNOWLEDGMENTS

I'd like to express my deep gratitude to those who have influenced and supported me in completing this third edition of *Exercising Influence*.

To my colleagues and partners at Barnes & Conti and our global affiliates— my deep appreciation for keeping the ideas and practices in the program and the book alive, fresh, and developing for all these years we have worked together. I'm grateful for your talent, commitment, and creativity every day.

To my writing group—in particular, to Bev Scott and Jan Schmuckler—many thanks for your help in shaping the new chapters. Your willingness to challenge my thinking and suggest resources was enormously helpful.

To the editors and other staff at John Wiley & Sons for making this as easy as it could be—your magic act of keeping a respectful distance, while being there when I needed something, helped this to come together faster than I thought possible.

To the thousands of people around the globe who have attended *Exercising Influence*™ workshops and put what they've learned into practice, your feedback and the gift of knowing about some of the great ideas you've moved into action inspire me every day.

And finally, to my family—especially to the other writers, daughters Heather Davis and Tamara Raetz, and my dear partner and husband, Don Bryant—my love and gratitude for being there, cheering me on, and keeping me grounded.

B. Kim Barnes
December, 2014

Exercising Influence

1

What We've Got Here Is a Failure to Influence

Dealing with Life 101

Shallow men believe in luck.

—Ralph Waldo Emerson

Do any of these situations sound familiar to you?

- It's five o'clock. You've been at your desk since six this morning, and you're nowhere near ready to go home. You have a meeting with your manager tomorrow morning, and you're supposed to have a report finished. You would have, too, if the other people involved had done their parts. First, the data was late from your counterpart in the other group. The people on your team had other priorities and couldn't help you with the analysis. Then the "admin" was too busy to help you prepare a decent-looking presentation. You might have asked your manager for an extension, but you didn't want to look unprepared, so you decided to do it all yourself. It looks like an all-nighter.

- Your teenage daughter, a bright and successful student, has announced that she will be turning down a scholarship to a prestigious university in favor

3

of taking a year off to travel and "find herself." You've had several heated arguments about this. Recently, you told her that you couldn't guarantee that you would pay her college tuition when she returned. Her response was that she was perfectly capable of earning her own money and attending a less expensive school. You feel that you've painted yourself into a corner and haven't made any progress in convincing her of the importance to her future of making the right college choice. You're also concerned about her safety as a solo traveler in certain parts of the world.

- You are a senior executive charged with the responsibility for implementing the final steps in merging two companies. Executives of the other firm, who see this as an acquisition by your company rather than a merger, are dragging their feet in regard to getting their systems aligned with yours. They give you excuses that sound rational, but the net effect is to delay the implementation. You're under a lot of pressure to get this completed. The new, merged systems should have been up and running by now, and you're feeling very frustrated and angry.

- You volunteered to help plan and host the yearly fund-raiser for your child's preschool. You were reluctant to take this on for fear that you might end up, as has happened before, doing it all yourself. The first few meetings of your committee were very positive; several people volunteered to take responsibility for specific tasks. Now it's two weeks before the event and several important things haven't happened. Everyone has an excuse for not delivering on his or her commitments. You feel that the staff and board are depending on you, and you don't want to let them down. This experience has convinced you, however, that you're not cut out for community leadership. You feel burned out and disappointed.

- You've been nurturing an idea for a couple of years now. It would be an application of your current technology that you believe would have a tremendous impact on the market. It would require a moderate commitment of resources, but the payoff could be spectacular. The problem is that such a project is outside of your current area of responsibility and, in fact, might be seen as competitive with another team's current project. Your manager has already told you that you would have to have it approved and funded elsewhere. You're beginning to suspect that it's a political "hot potato." You're still hoping that someone will recognize the potential and support it, but feel discouraged.

- You were recently offered an exciting new position with your company. It would involve spending three years abroad and would probably lead to a significant role for you in the company's future. When you told your spouse about it, you expected enthusiastic support. Instead, you received a flat and resistant response. This surprised you, as you have always agreed that whichever one of you was offered the best opportunity would have the other's support, regardless of any inconvenience and disruption that might occur.

- You lead an important project for your company. The project is not going as well as you had hoped. There's a lot of conflict, and milestones are not being achieved. You were selected for this role because of your technical skills, but you're feeling dragged down by the day-to-day hassle of dealing with people's egos and working out the turf issues that seem to get in the way of every cross-functional team you have worked with.

- You chair a standards task force for your association that could have a major impact on the conduct of your profession. Some members of the group are very resistant to the idea of mandatory compliance with the standards. You and several others believe that it's an exercise in futility to develop and present standards and then let people choose whether to adopt them or not. The differences have divided the group, which has now reached an impasse. If you can't come to an agreement, the entire exercise will be seen as a waste of time. You're concerned that you might lose the respect of your colleagues, both within the task force and outside of it, as they've been counting on you to resolve this issue.

The Value of Influence Skills

If you have ever experienced anything like the situations above, you know that all of your technical competence and skills won't resolve the human issues involved in getting business or personal results that are important to you and others. In the real world, a good idea doesn't necessarily sell itself. People don't always share the same values, priorities, and vested interests, even though they work for the same company, share a profession, or live in the same community or household. If you want to be successful as a leader, manager, colleague, friend, spouse, parent, or partner, you must be able to achieve results through the effort and support of others. This requires a good set of influence skills. You already know a lot about influence—we all use it and are affected by the way others use it. By reading this book, practicing, and reflecting, you will bring the process of influence to your conscious attention and learn to manage it with greater focus, precision, ease, and effectiveness.

As a business or technical leader, you are charged with the responsibility for getting results through others—frequently those over whom you don't exercise direct control. Although this is a common expectation, you may not have received any training or preparation for the tough issues and challenges that come with this territory.

As a member of a team, family, club, or other small group, you know that these groups seldom operate on the basis of hierarchical power or seniority (though you might sometimes wish they would, especially if you are a parent, a commit-tee chair, or a team leader). You may not have many role models for influencing effectively in this kind of environment.

Skillful influencing is more than just effective communication. It's possible to communicate often and clearly without achieving your desired results. Influence skills can be learned, but success as an influencer also requires you to have the abil-ity to read the person and the situation—and the discipline to hold a clear goal in mind while selecting and using the behaviors that are likely to lead you toward that goal. There are many opportunities in daily life to exercise your influence.

A good set of influence skills can lead to

- Improved ability to manage and lead cross-functionally
- More positive and productive personal and professional relationships
- Greater ability to choose and use behaviors tactically to achieve strategic objectives
- More confidence in your ability to achieve results through other people and a better track record of actually doing so
- Increased flexibility in dealing with people from diverse professional and cul-tural backgrounds, as well as those who differ from you in gender, generation, experience, and personality
- Improved skills for resolving conflict

Influence involves sophisticated understandings and a complex set of skills. Some situations are fairly straightforward and require little in the way of plan-ning; others are Byzantine in their complexity. We don't always get to choose which influence opportunities we'll be confronted with. In this book, we'll explore some practical ideas and tools for exercising influence in all aspects of your life. We'll examine recent research about how people respond to influence and how they make decisions. I've tried to cover, at least briefly, the major areas that are useful for the influencer to explore. Not all of them will be relevant to or needed for every influence situation. I hope you'll find enough here to stimulate your interest in influence and increase your confidence as an influencer. The best way to learn it, of course, is to do it.

What Is Influence, and Why Do We Want to Have It?

The Upside and the Downside

All that Adam had, all that Caesar could, you have and can do. . . . Build, therefore, your own world.

—Ralph Waldo Emerson

Influence and Power

The word *power* is a noun that indicates ability, strength, and authority. *Influence* is most often used as a verb, meaning to sway or induce another to take action. (It can also be used as a noun, often interchangeably with power.) In this book, we'll consider power to be something you *have* and influence to be something you *do*. Electric power exists only as a potential source of light in your home or office until you flip a switch (or activate an app or a beam that does the switching). Likewise, your power exists only as potential until you activate it through the use of influence.

7

Many sources of power are available to you. Among them are

- Formal authority associated with your role, job, or office
- Referred or delegated power from a person or a group that you represent
- Information, skill, or expertise
- Reputation for achievements and ability to get things done
- Relationships and mutual obligations
- Moral authority, based on the respect and admiration of others for the way that you act on your principles
- Personal power, based on self-confidence and commitment to an idea

Power may be used directly (for example, "You are going to bed now because I am your mother and I say so") or indirectly, through others (for example, "Let Jack know in a subtle way that I would prefer the other vendor"). If the demanding party's power is understood and considered legitimate and sufficient from the point of view of the responding party, the action will happen. In general, when power is called for, it's better to use it directly to avoid confusion, delay, or doubt. Power used indirectly can sometimes be experienced as manipulation, because most of us define manipulation as an attempt to influence in a false or obscure way.

Many situations call for the direct use of power. Emergencies and other situations in which rapid decision making is essential are times when fast and effective action is more important than involvement and commitment.

In day-to-day life, the direct use of power has several limitations

- Others must perceive your power as legitimate, sufficient, and appropriate to the situation.
- The use of power seldom changes minds or hearts; thus you can't count on follow-up that you are not there to supervise.
- The direct use of power doesn't invite others to take a share of the responsibility for the outcome. Others don't have the opportunity to grow by having to make decisions and live with the consequences.

Influence behavior instead uses your sources of power to move another person toward making a conscious choice or commitment that supports a goal you wish to achieve. Different sources of power will be appropriate with different people and in different situations. They will support the use of a variety of influence skills. Using influence rather than direct power sends a message of respect to the other. It results in action by the other that is voluntary rather than coerced; thus quality and timelines are likely to be better. It's also the realistic choice to make in the many situations we encounter in which we need to get things done through people over whom we have no legitimate power.

Influence and Leadership

Leaders must be able to use both approaches—direct power and skillful influencing—and must know when each is appropriate. Few leaders are satisfied with blind obedience (obedience in adults is never "blind"—it's an emergency response, a fear response, or one that betrays a lack of interest in and responsibility for the outcome). Most leaders want to work with people who are willing to influence as well as to be influenced.

Because influence tends to be reciprocal, part of a relationship, it's important for a leader to let others know when and how he or she can be influenced on an issue. A big mistake often made by leaders and managers is to act as if they can be influenced (for example, by asking people what they think about something) and then communicating (often by arguing with their suggestions) that the decision has already been made. Presumably, the leader was hoping that people would come to the same—obvious to the leader—conclusion so that they would be committed to the decision. This only creates cynicism and has given "participatory management" and "employee empowerment" bad names.

If you need to use direct power, use it with confidence, not apologetically. Then involve people about something related to the issue where you can be influenced. For example, suppose that a reorganization will occur whether your direct reports want it to happen or not. Although you might be tempted to try to develop support for the action by seeming to engage others in the decision, you know that would be inappropriate given the fact that the decision has already been made. Announce it and give people time to absorb the news, express concerns, and ask questions. Then ask, "What support will you need from me to communicate about this and plan transitions for your employees?"

Successful leaders learn and practice a wide variety of influence behaviors. They keep the goal in front of them and act in a way that is consistent with the aim of achieving that result, through and with others. Leadership in a team, family, or community organization is usually shared. The option to use direct power is often less available or effective, yet the responsibilities remain. Those in both formal and informal leadership roles must call on their personal influence skills to align other members toward a shared goal and to energize and inspire them to do what it takes to achieve it.

Your Sphere of Influence

Each of us has a "sphere of influence." This includes issues and areas over which we exercise control, those where we can directly influence the outcome, and those where we can influence the situation indirectly through other people or as part of a group.

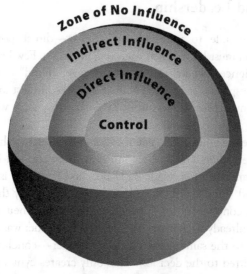

Figure 2.1   Sphere of Influence.

Use Figure 2.1 to chart your current sphere of influence. In which aspects of your life can you control an outcome by yourself? Where can you directly influence someone to take an action that you need or prefer? Where do you have the opportunity to influence a situation indirectly by getting another person or a group to do the direct influence? What are the areas and issues in your life that are important to you, but where you see no opportunity to influence?

Many people find that their areas of direct control are limited to choices about their own behavior, but that it's possible to influence, either directly or indirectly, many events and outcomes in which they hold a strong interest. As you review your chart, notice how active a role you are taking in influencing the outcome of issues and events that you care about. Is there anything about which you care deeply that you perceive as being outside of your sphere of influence entirely?

Typical examples for sphere of control might include

- What to wear (what is "business casual," anyway?)
- The order in which you do certain things
- The level of your own commitment
- How to organize your workspace or closet
- Your own behavioral choices, for example, how to communicate with or influence someone

These are choices you can make on your own—no one else needs to be involved or consulted (although you may opt to involve or consult others).

Your sphere of direct influence may include issues involving

- Family members
- Friends
- Manager or project leader
- Team members
- Peers
- Direct reports
- Mentors or project sponsors
- Internal and external customers
- Neighbors
- Vendors
- Neighborhood business owners
- Local government officials
- Local media
- Members and leaders of professional and community organizations of which you are a member

In these cases, you can go directly to the person or group you wish to influence and use your skills to achieve the results that are of interest to you.

Your sphere of indirect influence may include

- Senior managers in your company
- Other department heads
- Regional and national government officials who represent you in some way
- Competitors
- The leadership of large companies with which you do business
- Your customers' customers
- The national media

You may be able to have an impact on them through others who are in a position to influence them directly. Alternatively, you might organize a group to influence together by initiating a campaign through social media or other means.

External events, trends, and issues can also have an important impact on our approach to influencing someone. Most of us would acknowledge that we have little or no influence in areas such as the global economy, a competitor's business strategy, large-scale trends such as industry consolidation, or decisions made by leaders of countries we don't live in, any more than we do the weather. Yet these and other decisions and events can have an impact on our lives and on how we influence. For example, knowing that a certain industry is having difficulty filling orders because of shortages of a raw material from a country that is at war may affect our approach to negotiating a business deal. We may not have any impact on the route a hurricane will take, but we can use information we have heard about it to influence a relative's travel plans. Trends, events, and other factors over which we have no control provide the *context* within which we exercise our influence.

Empowerment: Buzzword or Reality?

In today's information-based organizations, direct power and control are rare commodities. Particularly in competitive, global organizations, decisions depend on complex information drawn from a variety of sources. Governance of the organization is often broad-based. Much of the work of these organizations occurs across functions, outside of formal hierarchies, frequently by teams of people who rarely, if ever, meet face-to-face. Increasingly, people who are empowered to take action make decisions across boundaries of space, time, and nationality.

If asked, most people would say they don't want control over other people—but neither do they want others to have control over them. Research on work-related stress has demonstrated that those with low power and high responsibility have the greatest levels of stress. Our physiological "fight-or-flight" response is intensified when we feel the pressure to take action but have neither the legitimacy nor the resources to make something happen. Organizations in which people feel they have little influence over matters that affect them become "cultures of complaint."

Although there has been much discussion in organizations and families about empowerment, the reality is that, as individuals and groups, we can't wait passively for others to give us power. Organizations, institutions, and leaders may offer us power, but we can use it only when we have created and accepted empowerment for ourselves. Accepting empowerment means accepting responsibility for the outcome of our actions. As a buzzword, empowerment has probably run its course—but as a concept, it has a lot of life left. In most organizations and families these days, true empowerment means an openness to influence from and in all directions.

Families today are less hierarchical. In North America, Australia, New Zealand, and much of Western and Central Europe, the typical family is a complex unit made up of individuals with a variety of sources of power and levels of responsibility. There is a greater variety of family constellations than ever before. Roles in the family are more fluid than in the past. Typically, more than one parent has a job or career. In single-parent families, where the parent is working, children may assume greater responsibilities. Traditional extended families are often less available or geographically convenient, especially in North America. Children may have information and economic power bases that enable them to participate in family decisions on a more equal basis than in the past, when parents and grandparents were keepers of traditions, knowledge, and authority. For example, when parents aren't "digital natives," and the children are, the power balance changes. Peer groups offer an alternative source of need satisfaction for children and adolescents, rendering the nuclear family less powerful, whether we like it or not.

In communities, also, the traditional power relationships in Western society have broken down. There is no overarching institution, like the church in medieval society or Tammany Hall in turn-of-the-twentieth-century New York, to provide the final word on what can and should be done. Instead, there are multiple competing interest groups, each with its own set of problems and preferred solutions. It sometimes seems that the community is divided into tiny fractions, each with a particular vested interest around which to organize. Yet, people from many cultural, religious, occupational, economic, and educational backgrounds must be able to come to agreement on solutions to problems that affect all of them.

In today's more open and empowered organizations and societies, opportunities for exerting influence and power abound for those who are willing to accept the attendant responsibilities and accountabilities.

Benefits and Costs of Exercising Influence

In this complex, multi-ethnic society, individuals must depend on their interpersonal skills to build coalitions and make things happen with and through the people within their spheres of influence. The benefits are clear — you can achieve goals that you couldn't accomplish by yourself and reduce the stress associated with having a lot of responsibility without sufficient resources to do the job. You can create visibility and opportunity for yourself and for ideas, causes, or projects that are important to you.

For example, you may be responsible at work or in your community for a project that has no budget. In order to achieve the results you hope for and are expected to accomplish, you'll have to beg, borrow, or steal the required resources. You'll need to influence the right people to take an interest in your project's success and be willing to contribute time, energy, equipment, people, or money to make it happen.

Or perhaps you'd like to purchase a vacation home, but you know that it will require some voluntary sacrifices on the part of everyone in the family to make it a reality. You may have to forego regular vacations for a couple of years. You'll have to influence the rest of the family to share your vision and trade off near-term pleasures for longer-term satisfaction.

I remember a client who called me in despair one day to report that he was near exhaustion; nobody seemed willing to help him complete a long report that was due the following week, and he didn't know how he was going to finish in time. I asked him what he had done to get some support from his teammates. He answered, "They can see that I'm over my head and nobody has offered to do a thing." "Yes," I said, "but have you asked them?" He allowed that he had not. The next day, he called back to report that everyone he had asked had been willing to do something. "They thought I didn't need help," he said, wonderingly.

This story illustrates an obvious benefit. Making the effort to influence can pay off in many ways. Still, choosing to exercise your influence can be costly in time and effort, and sometimes in other, more subtle ways. Once we've become active in influencing a particular outcome, we may create expectations on the part of others that we will continue to champion certain ideas and values. By taking an active role, we may also face more in the way of conflict and feel that we have to accept greater responsibility. It's always useful to balance the costs and benefits when deciding whether to put forth the energy required to influence.

Where Should We Exercise Influence?

Although some issues at work, at home, and in community activities are appropriately handled through the use of direct power or simple communication, many others lend themselves particularly well to influence. Influence issues are ones that require mutual agreement and commitment.

Typical workplace influence issues include

- Getting support for ideas
- Assigning responsibilities in a team
- Acquiring needed resources for a project
- Being assigned to interesting projects or career development opportunities

Some family or household issues that lend themselves well to influence include

- Distributing chores, tasks, and responsibilities
- Planning for vacations or outings
- Assigning proportions of costs for shared activities or household expenses
- Making decisions about major purchases

In community activities, almost everything is subject to influence, because most people are volunteering their time. Examples include

- Convincing the right people to serve on a committee
- Gaining agreement on principles and processes
- Getting people to deliver on commitments
- Managing disagreements and conflicts

Developing and Improving Influence Fitness

All of us learn early in our lives how to influence the people who are most important to our well-being. As infants, we have only a few means of communicating our needs and wants. Gradually, we develop a complete set of influence muscles. Toddlers experiment with a wide variety of means to exert influence. Through observation, education, experience, and experimentation, we tend to develop a favored set of influence skills—ones that we have been most exposed to or that have worked best for us. As long as we remain within the context (family, culture, school, workplace) where we've been successful as influencers, there's little need to develop some of the underused or rejected skills. However, when we embark on new experiences, encounter new problems, or meet new people, we may find that our present levels of expertise won't allow us the flexibility we need to be successful.

In our influence skills workshops, we view developing influence skills as analogous to developing physical fitness. You have all the muscles you'll ever need, but a good fitness program helps you build and develop them, so you can be more powerful, graceful, and flexible—in greater control of your own physical and mental well-being. Similarly, you already have all the basic influence muscles you need, but some of them are probably underdeveloped or flabby due to lack of use. A purposeful program for developing influence fitness can also enable you to become more powerful, graceful, and flexible—more effective as a person at work, at home, and in your community.

Reading this book can introduce you to the concepts involved in conscious and effective influencing, especially if you do so with specific influence opportunities in mind. But only by practicing the behaviors in a safe environment, where you can count on receiving honest feedback, will you truly develop those influence muscles.

(See Appendix A for some suggestions about setting up a coaching partnership.)

CHAPTER 3

A Model for Exercising Influence

Building Relationships and Getting Results

The life of [a person] is a self-evolving circle, which, from a ring imperceptibly small, rushes on all sides outward to new and larger circles, and that without end. The extent to which this generation of circles . . . will go depends on the force or truth of the individual soul.

—Ralph Waldo Emerson

A Framework for Influence

Influencing others successfully is a complex process. It's not enough to be interpersonally skillful. There's nothing you can do or say that will guarantee success every time with every person in every situation. However, you can help yourself to succeed in challenging influence situations like the ones described at the beginning of this book by considering the entire framework of your

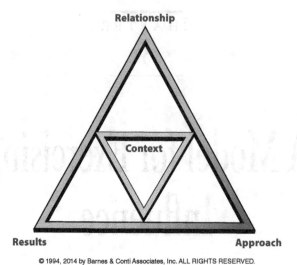

Figure 3.1   Influence Framework.

influence opportunity. Figure 3.1 represents an effective framework for thinking about influence. There are four elements within the framework

1. *Results:* What are you hoping to accomplish through influencing this person?
2. *Relationship:* What kind of influence relationship do you currently have?
3. *Context:* What individual, organizational, or cultural issues might affect the results?
4. *Approach:* Which influence tactics and behaviors are most likely to help you accomplish your goal?

This chapter will give you an overview of each of the elements in the influence framework. In Part II, each of these elements will be developed more fully, with suggestions as to how you can apply the information to a real influence opportunity.

Results: What Would Success Look Like?

When thinking about an influence opportunity, the best place to start is where you would like to end up. What result do you hope to achieve by influencing this person or group? How will you know that you have been successful? What will you see, hear, or experience that will let you know you've accomplished your goal? What specific influence objectives will you need to achieve along the way?

Sometimes we're embarrassed or ashamed to acknowledge, even to ourselves, that we want results—pretty specific results at that—and will be deeply disappointed if we don't obtain them. When we don't approve of our own wish to influence, we might be manipulative or halfhearted about the process, hoping to get away with it without anyone—even ourselves—noticing. And, of course, that doesn't work very well. So if you care about the outcome of a discussion, a meeting, a proposal, a request, or a family council, let yourself know it. When you can do this, you've started along the path of conscious influencing. You won't always be successful, but you'll probably find that you feel stronger, less stressed, and more powerful because you're taking an active role rather than playing the victim of circumstances or of other people's actions or decisions.

Influence goals (long-term) and objectives (short-term) are based on needs and requirements that can often be met in a variety of ways. Sometimes you'll change your specific influence objective in order to be more certain of achieving a long-term result that will meet your needs. In Chapter 8, you will learn how to design an influence objective that will be a good "star to steer by."

Relationship: How Well Do You Influence One Another?

A key element in your influence framework is the relationship you've developed with the person you wish to influence. An influence relationship exists, potentially, when one or both parties have goals that require the support or actions of the other. Not all relationships are influence relationships. There are people with whom we communicate regularly, but whose actions are irrelevant to our own goals. It's possible to have a good friendship with someone without having an effective influence relationship with him or her, and it's possible to have a good influence relationship with someone you wouldn't choose as a friend. Because influencing another person is not an event, but rather part of a process, everything that occurs in your influence relationship affects the future of that relationship. The success or failure of subsequent influence opportunities with that person depends on the influence history you build together. If the other person or group feels that you were unfair or dishonest, you will become less influential. In other words, every time you influence someone, you make it easier or more difficult to influence that person the next time.

When you assess the state of an influence relationship honestly and accurately, you'll probably know whether or not the other person is likely to be open to your influence. If not, you'll have to begin by doing the work that's required to repair or rebuild your influence relationship—or decide to influence indirectly through another person or group.

An influence relationship at work or in the community is not necessarily a close personal friendship. You may have few social interests in common or have the wrong chemistry to be friends. The basic criterion for choosing someone with whom to build an influence relationship is that there is some mutual benefit possible if you are willing and able to help or support one another.

In this complex and changing world, building solid and mutually beneficial influence relationships within your organization and profession, as well as outside of it, creates a network of information and opportunity that you'll be able to call on throughout your professional life. Building positive influence relationships in your family and community will provide you with a lifelong base of support. Paradoxically, the very moment that you need a good influence relationship the most is likely to be the hardest time to start building one. Successful influencers are aware of this; not only do they avoid burning bridges they may need to cross one day, but they put effort into building bridges before they are needed.

Chapter 9 will help you to better understand and to build and improve on your existing influence relationships. You'll also gain some ideas on developing new and effective influence relationships.

Context: What Else Is Going On?

Influence doesn't occur in a vacuum. There are always many factors in a situation that can affect the outcome. In general, these factors can be found in three areas.

1. Individual (both yourself and the person you want to influence)
   - *Personality and preferences:* Where is the "comfort zone" for each of us? How does he or she prefer to be influenced? What's my usual approach?
   - *Values and goals:* What is important to each of us? What's riding on this influence opportunity?
   - *Current issues and priorities:* Where is the other's attention focused right now? Is this a good time to influence?
   - *Needs and vested interests:* What does each of us have to gain or lose by the outcome?
2. Organizational
   - *Purpose and vision:* What's the organization about? How can I align my influence issue with organizational goals?
   - *Structure and processes:* How does the organization work? What do I need to know in order to get a hearing?
   - *Power relationships:* What are the current politics of the organization? Who is important to the success of my influence opportunity?
   - *Current issues and priorities:* What's important right now? How can I use that to increase the relevance of my approach?

3. Cultural (national, professional, community, or organizational)
   - *Values:* What does the nation, organization, or group believe to be right, good, or important? What are their criteria for decision making?
   - *Norms:* What's the "right way" to get things done?
   - *Taboos:* What's outside the boundaries of the acceptable?

Of course, influence doesn't take place within a closed system. External elements such as trends and issues in the environment may also have an impact on the outcome. These contextual elements, over which you have no control, may lead you to change or adapt your approach or timing.

You'll also want to spend some time thinking about how your own needs and vested interests, personality, and behavioral skills affect the context for influence with this particular person, organization, and/or culture. Chapters 10, 11, and 12 treat these issues in more depth and provide ideas and practical suggestions for dealing with each aspect of the context for influence.

Approach: How Will I Achieve Results?

Once you've established a realistic but optimistic objective, considered the state of the relationship, and analyzed the contextual factors, you're in a good position to select the tactical approach and specific behaviors that are most likely to accomplish the results you hope to achieve.

Direct influence behaviors fall into two categories: *expressive* influence and *receptive* influence. Expressive influence behaviors involve sending ideas and

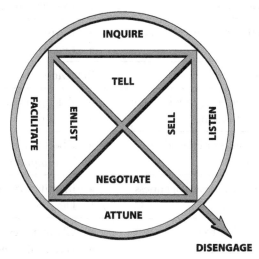

Figure 3.2   Influence Model.

information toward others in a way that will engage their interest and persuade them to support you. Receptive influence behaviors involve drawing ideas and information from others in a way that will guide them toward a commitment to action. The influence model in Figure 3.2 shows the expressive and receptive influence tactics.

Neither type of influence behavior is better or worse than the other one. Each of the behaviors is intended to accomplish a particular influence result. Used thoughtfully, in combination, they can lead you toward achieving your influence goals. Over time, often within the same conversation, you will aim to balance expressive and receptive influence energy. (In Chapter 14, you will learn some guidelines for selecting and using specific behaviors.)

Table 3.1 shows influence tactics and behaviors and what they're designed to accomplish. You'll notice two columns: tactics and behaviors. The *intention* is

Table 3.1   Influence Tactics and Behavior.

Expressive Tactics	Behaviors
Tell: Communicate the desired action	• Suggest • Express needs
Sell: Convince the other to commit to action	• Offer reasons • Refer to goals and benefits
Negotiate: Give the other a vested interest in taking action	• Offer incentives • Describe consequences
Enlist: Create enthusiasm and alignment	• Envision • Encourage
Receptive Tactics	**Behaviors**
Inquire: Get information or involvement; guide the other's thinking	• Ask open-ended questions • Draw out
Listen: Learn real limits or expand the other's thinking	• Check understanding • Test implications
Attune: Build trust or increase openness	• Identify with other • Disclose
Facilitate: Get the other to take responsibility for action	• Clarify issues • Pose challenging questions
Disengage	• Live to influence another day

what you want your behavior to achieve. The *tactic* is a summary of the intention. The *behaviors* are specific ways of implementing the tactics.

Influence behaviors have both verbal and nonverbal components. Facial expression, voice tone, gestures, and the way you use physical or virtual space can all contribute to or detract from the impact of your influence.

Using any influence behavior effectively requires, first of all, being clear about the results you want to obtain—your influence goal. Next, you'll think about the person you intend to influence and the influence relationship you currently have with one another. You'll consider the context in which the influence will take place: individual, team, organizational, cultural, or external factors and issues that might affect the outcome. You can then select the tactics and behaviors that are most likely to be useful under the circumstances and even plan a specific approach. During the actual influence event, you'll stay alert to the other's responses and monitor whether you're moving closer to or further from your goal—or approaching an alternate result that meets your needs satisfactorily. You may stick with your plan, modify it based on the other's response, or disengage to rethink your approach.

In Chapters 4 and 5, you'll explore the specific influence behaviors in greater depth. In Chapter 14, you'll learn how to choose and use influence behaviors to achieve specific results.

What Is the Issue?

Some influence opportunities are focused on personal preferences and priorities. Some, however, involve deep and complex issues that require study and exploration. Influence opportunities that are related to a specific problem that's owned or shared by the other person may require you to develop a thorough understanding of the issues involved. Chapter 13 provides some suggestions as to how to prepare for influence situations that involve complex issues.

Expressive Influence

Sending Ideas and Generating Energy

Nothing great was ever accomplished without enthusiasm.
— Ralph Waldo Emerson

The Purpose of Expressive Influence

Expressive influence sends your ideas and energy out to others. Many people think of influence as primarily an expressive activity — one in which they're continually sending ideas and information toward others. In fact, effective influence requires a balance of expressive and receptive activity, as does any form of communication.

Too many people overuse or misuse expressive influence. On the one hand, you've probably been in meetings where long-windedness, repetitiveness, a sleep-inducing slide presentation, and/or an excruciating level of detail caused you to leave the meeting mentally or physically without absorbing or being influenced by a single idea. There was probably little or no opportunity to ask a question or make a comment that might have sparked a productive discussion. Virtual attendees were ignored. Often, the speaker involved in such a meeting is unaware of his or her impact (or lack of it) because he or she is focused internally on what to say next, rather than attending to whether or not the current words are having an impact.

On the other hand, you may have had the good fortune to listen to someone who stimulated your thinking with an exciting idea, changed your mind through an excellent argument, made you an offer you didn't want to refuse, or inspired you to believe that you could accomplish great things.

Expressive influence, used effectively, can lead people to action. It's especially effective when people are uncertain about what to do and have respect for and trust in the person who is influencing. The use of expressive influence can communicate to others that you mean business and are to be taken seriously. It allows you to communicate your enthusiasm for an idea or belief and exhort others to share it.

The Expressive Behaviors

Figure 4.1 shows the specific tactics and behaviors associated with expressive influence. The expressive tactics in this model are named according to what they are intended to do. They include *Tell*, *Sell*, *Negotiate*, and *Enlist*.

1. You can *Tell* by making a suggestion or by expressing your needs.
   - "Let's meet twice a month on the standards issue until we're ready to present the report." (*Suggest*)
   - "I need your input on the plans by Friday." (*Express needs*)

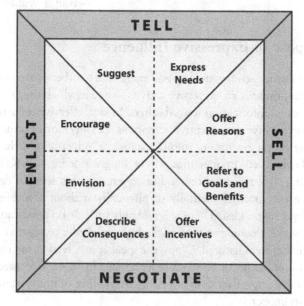

Figure 4.1   Expressive Influence Tactics and Behaviors.

2. You can *Sell* by offering reasons or by referring to goals and benefits.
   - "That way, we can meet the deadline for the report." (*Offer reasons*)
   - "With both of us contributing, we should be able to achieve our goal of completing the plan before the end of the quarter." (*Refer to goals and benefits*)

3. You can *Negotiate* by offering incentives or by describing consequences.
   - "If you'll extend the deadline by a week, I'll provide you with an outline of the major conclusions that you can use for your meeting." (*Offer incentives*)
   - "I need to let you know that if you're not ready by seven o'clock tomorrow, I won't be available to drive you to school." (*Describe consequences*)

4. You can *Enlist* by envisioning a desired future or by encouraging the other person to join you.
   - "I can see our team creating the product that finally puts this company on the map." (*Envision*)
   - "You're exactly the person who can attract the best candidate. You have a special ability to communicate the exciting work we want to do here." (*Encourage*)

How Expressive Behaviors Work

- *Tell* behaviors influence by letting others know what you want and need from them. Often, people will be willing to help and support your efforts if they know what you'd like them to do.
- *Sell* behaviors influence by showing people reasons for and benefits from taking an action.
- *Negotiate* behaviors influence by offering others a fair exchange for taking or refraining from taking an action.
- *Enlist* behaviors influence by creating enthusiasm and putting the other "in the picture."

Nonverbal Components of Expressive Behaviors

Expressive gestures, at least in Western cultures, are confident, free, and direct (although pointing your finger at someone while speaking will be perceived as aggressive and should be avoided). Try not to tilt your head while using these behaviors; it's a basic mammalian signal indicating, "I acknowledge your superiority." (Watch the neighborhood dogs as they work out the hierarchy. We do the same thing, only we're a little subtler about it.) Smiling while using *Tell, Sell,* or

Negotiate behaviors can indicate uncertainty and nervousness. (Smiling is a natural and appropriate expression of enthusiasm while enlisting.) Eye contact should be used carefully with expressive influence. Too much of it may be perceived as challenging and aggressive. Direct eye contact is best used at key points, when you want to add emphasis. The rest of the time, you can look at the other person's forehead or cheekbones. This is polite, but not invasive.

Your posture should be relaxed but erect and balanced. My aikido teacher once pointed out that the Japanese concept of "hara" or center was physically located in a space about two inches below your navel. He said that you should feel your weight centered there. If you're centered in your chest, you'll seem aggressive; if in your head, placating. Keep both feet on the floor. (I know your fourth-grade teacher told you this. Do it anyway; it makes you look and sound much more confident. Try it.) These suggestions can make a difference even on the phone or in a virtual meeting where the other can't see you—having more confident posture can translate into more confident expression. Standing up can add to your effectiveness face-to-face, especially if you're physically smaller than the person or people you're influencing. Using a flip chart or whiteboard can make this a natural part of the discussion.

Your voice should come from as low as possible in your register; breathing helps. The emotional (and vocal) tone that works with expressive influence is businesslike and matter-of-fact, unless you are enlisting the other. For that purpose, you'll use more colorful language and variable inflection. A sarcastic, negative, or hostile tone is likely to create a defensive reaction in the other person, who will conclude that you're not interested in two-way influence. Ending a sentence with an upward inflection may indicate uncertainty or a lack of confidence in what you're expressing, at least in some societies. (This may account for some misunderstandings between Canadians, who often use that inflection conversationally, and other English speakers.)

Using Expressive Influence at Work

Expressive influence is particularly useful at work early in a project or process, whether as part of a one-to-one conversation or in a meeting. The most obvious use of expressive behavior at work is simply to let others know what you want or need them to do. A good deal of time could be saved in most organizations if we were clearer with one another about this. Unfortunately, we're often reluctant to ask directly for what we want—sometimes because we're not sure it's legitimate to ask for it, sometimes because we don't want to hear a direct "no," and sometimes because we don't want the implicit or explicit responsibilities that would accompany an open agreement.

Meetings can be dull and unproductive when participants are unwilling to express opinions and ideas. This may happen because of hidden conflict or fear of upsetting the status quo. People are also sometimes afraid to express ideas because of political or cultural concerns about whether they have the right to speak up and whether others will listen. Meetings that are consciously designed to stimulate a balance of expressive and receptive behaviors are most likely to be productive. (See Appendix C for suggested meeting process designs.)

Many conflicts in organizations arise because we're not explicit in expressing our needs and then become upset when we don't get what we want. We leave meetings with an idea of who will do what by when, but then we find that others interpreted the agreement differently. We do several favors for a colleague, believing that he or she "owes us one," but when we try to collect a return favor, we find that the other person has been keeping a different set of accounts. We believe strongly in a course of action and are deeply disappointed when we can't convince or inspire others to join us.

All of these issues might have been prevented by the thoughtful use of expressive influence behavior, for example:

- "I'd like you to meet with me every week to review progress." (*Express needs*)
- "By participating, your team will gain greater visibility with our client." (*Refer to goals and benefits*)
- "I'd be glad to spend a day training your assistant on that. In exchange, I'd like you to assign him to our team for a day next week to help us complete our project." (*Offer incentives*)
- "If I don't have your numbers by Friday, I won't have time to include them in the report." (*Describe consequences*)
- "Here's what I see as possible. Six months from now we're all able to find every piece of data we need within minutes because we've agreed on a single database system that will work for all of us." (*Envision*)

Using Expressive Influence at Home

At home, the use of expressive influence is often complicated by the thought, "I shouldn't have to tell him or her that." We sometimes act as though mind reading is a test of familial devotion. Psychologists have introduced us to the concept of the "double bind." ("I don't want you to clean up your room. I want you to *want* to clean up your room.") In a double-bind situation, whichever choice you make is going to be the wrong one. If the child cleans up at the parent's request, that will not meet the parent's need—nor, of course, will ignoring the request.

Using conscious and effective influence behavior at home is a good antidote to the complexities of family or household communication. A good influence goal (see Chapter 8) has to be observable in the short term, so you know when you're on the right track or whether it would be better to take another approach. You can hear whether or not your housemate, son, or daughter has committed to clean the room. And you can see quite shortly afterward whether the room is clean (if you don't look in the closets or under the bed). And you'll probably learn to be pretty satisfied with that, because it cuts down on a lot of unproductive conflict and aggravation.

- "I'd like you to help me with the yard work this morning." (*Express needs*)
- "There are two benefits for taking some long weekends rather than our usual vacation this summer. First, that will allow us to save enough to buy a boat for next summer, and second, I'll have enough vacation days left for us to take a skiing vacation this winter." (*Refer to goals and benefits*—assuming the other is interested in either the boat or the ski vacation.)
- "If you'll agree to get a job that will pay for your room and board, I'll take responsibility for tuition and books." (*Offer incentives*)
- "It's a tough situation, but I see you as the kind of person who can inspire your peers to do the right thing. I remember how you got them to support the volunteer program." (*Encourage*)

Using Expressive Influence in Your Community

In community organizations, people are often not being paid to do the work that we want them to do or to take the stand that we wish they would. We may err on the side of vagueness rather than sound as if we are trying to be "the boss." Knowing that the only rewards for volunteer work in community service or religious organizations or political action groups are intangible satisfactions and others' appreciation, we tend to "go easy," rather than risk the loss of support and help. This can lead to a lack of energy and direction in the group or organization.

- "I believe in this project, and I'm willing to take responsibility for getting us started. Now I need two people who will work with me, starting today." (*Express needs*)
- "Maria's credentials are an exact match with our criteria." (*Offer reasons*)

- "If you're not willing to agree to put our name out there in support of this initiative, I'll lose respect for this organization—and I believe that others will, too." (*Describe consequences*)
- "Here's what I anticipate. We're going to emerge from this crisis as a strong, united team, ready to lead this organization in an exciting new direction." (*Envision*)

When to Use Expressive Behaviors

As stated earlier, expressive and receptive behaviors work together, not in isolation from one another. Overall, you'll strive for a balance of the two. Each kind of behavior has value and accomplishes certain specific results.

In summary, use expressive influence behaviors at work, at home, and in your community when

- You want people to know what you need
- You have a solution to a problem that has been expressed by the other
- The conversation does not seem to be going anywhere
- You want to generate enthusiasm and energy
- You want to bring disagreements out in the open
- You want to move toward completing an agreement or gaining a commitment

Learning to be clear, direct, and straightforward in your expressive influence takes courage and confidence. It's easiest when you do your homework, considering both facts and legitimate needs. It's also important that you be as prepared to listen respectfully to others' opinions and ideas as you hope they are to listen to yours. In the next chapter, you'll learn about the behaviors that will help you to do this.

Receptive Influence

Inviting Ideas and Stimulating Action

Explore and explore. Be neither chided nor flattered out of your position of perpetual inquiry. Neither dogmatize [nor] accept another's dogmatism.
—Ralph Waldo Emerson

The Purpose of Receptive Influence

Receptive influence invites others to contribute ideas, information, and commitment to action. Since most people tend to overuse expressive behaviors when they wish to influence, they also tend to underuse receptive behaviors—behaviors that they may use very effectively and unself-consciously as part of everyday conversations with friends and family, in coaching or counseling sessions, or in intellectual discussions. It's not obvious to everyone that receptive behaviors offer an effective way to influence others directly.

Receptive behaviors, used skillfully, can guide you and others toward an agreement, solution, or choice that satisfies each of you. You can't really influence a person to do something that he or she knows to be against his or her best interests, because influence implies choice, unless you are appealing to a negative and vulnerable aspect of that person. (This is discussed in Chapter 16 on the ethics of influence.)

Receptive influence indicates respect for the ideas and concerns of the other person and acknowledges his or her authority and accountabilities. At the same time, it creates a channel for the conversation that is flexible, yet goal-directed. This is how it differs from using similar communication behaviors when you don't have a goal in mind, where your intention may simply be to gather information or to assist another person in solving his or her own problem. As an influencer, you are consciously and openly moving toward a goal. You know that the other person has to go there with you willingly, so you make it easier for him or her to move in that direction.

In his book, *To Sell Is Human*, Daniel Pink cites research on "perspective-taking," that is, getting inside the mind of the other person. He explains that the difference between perspective-taking and empathy is that perspective-taking is about thinking and empathy is about emotions. He describes research by Adam Galinsky, William Maddux, and others. They conducted a challenging negotiation simulation in which one third of the subjects were told to imagine how the other side was feeling (empathizing), one third to imagine what the other side was thinking (perspective-taking), and the third group acted as a control with general instructions. Both of the first two groups did better at creating good agreements for both parties than the control group, but the group that was given the perspective-taking instruction did significantly better.

Just as expressive behavior can be used in a way that disempowers others, receptive behaviors can be used in a manipulative way by someone acting as if he or she has no agenda, but behaving in a way that makes it clear that one exists (see Chapter 16). This is an ineffective and dishonest use of receptive behavior. It seldom works very well the first time, and it most certainly will not work a second time. As the saying goes, "Fool me once, shame on you—fool me twice, shame on me!"

Phrasing a statement as a question doesn't mean that it will be perceived as receptive behavior. Others will experience questions that present a position or suggest that there is a right answer, as *Tell* behaviors. For example, "What does your father always say about that?" is another way of saying, "You'd better do what Dad tells you to do." Questions that include the phrases, "Don't you think...?" or "Do you agree...?" are almost always expressive in nature and thus in impact. Leaders and managers are often surprised to learn that employees didn't feel involved in a decision, because they believed themselves to be inquiring and soliciting employees' ideas. This usually occurs when the subtext is a clear *Tell* message. The right, or politically wise, answer was clear. We are very good, as a species, at figuring this out.

Because receptive guidance must be light, rather than heavy, in order to be effective, it is essential that the influencer adopt a neutral, nonjudgmental point of view. If questions and comments promote—even subtly—the influencer's point of view, they will be treated, correctly, as expressive statements. People sometimes misuse receptive influence behaviors in the hope that they will not be caught influencing (see Chapter 16) and that the other person will believe that the result was his or her idea. This virtually never works. Most people are sensitive to having "words put into their mouths" and will not be fooled or coerced into commitment. They may "go along to get along." Many managers mistake their direct reports' politically expedient behavior for evidence of their own superior leadership and influence.

Because of the nature of receptive influence, it's almost never a one-way process. In drawing out and learning about the other person, the influencer will adapt and adjust and develop new ideas—sometimes even changing the influence goal as a result of new information. Often, effective receptive influence behavior provides an opportunity for both participants to accomplish important goals.

The Receptive Behaviors

Receptive behaviors include *Inquire*, *Listen*, *Attune*, and *Facilitate* (Figure 5.1).

1. You can *Inquire* by asking open-ended questions (ones that can't be answered by "yes" or "no") and by drawing the other person out.
   - "Where should we consider going on our vacation this year?" (*Ask open-ended questions*)
   - "You mentioned that you were uncomfortable with the direction we're taking. Tell me more about your thinking." (*Draw out*)
2. You can *Listen* by checking understanding and by testing implications of what the other has said.
   - "So from your point of view, that contractor has too little experience with custom-designed homes for you to feel comfortable." (*Check understanding*)
   - "I'm sensing that you're pretty hot under the collar about that." (*Test implications*)
3. You can *Attune* by identifying with the other person and disclosing information about yourself.
   - "If I were you, I might well be concerned about whether that would affect my eligibility." (*Identify with other*)
   - "I didn't listen to your ideas very well the last time we discussed this." (*Disclose*)

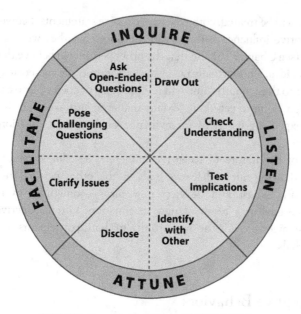

Figure 5.1   Receptive Influence Tactics and Behaviors.

4. You can *Facilitate* by clarifying issues and posing challenging questions.

   - "It seems that you're caught between wanting to be a good team player and feeling strongly that your idea is the only successful way to go." (*Clarify issues*)

   - "What would it take for you to be willing to put off the trip for a year?" (*Pose challenging questions*)

How Receptive Behaviors Work

- *Inquire* behaviors influence by establishing the topic, the issues, and the questions to be explored. In addition to providing information, they can encourage people to think along new lines, to consider new questions, and to deepen and expand their thinking about specific issues. This creates an opening for influence.

- *Listen* behaviors influence by clarifying, selecting, and emphasizing key areas of interest to both parties.

- *Attune* behaviors influence by creating an atmosphere of trust and common ground between the influencer and the other person. We are most likely to be influenced by people whom we trust.

- *Facilitate* behaviors influence by creating a bias toward action on the part of the other person. We are more likely to take action when someone we respect assumes we will, believes we can, and gives us just a slight push off the fence.

Nonverbal Components of Receptive Behaviors

Being receptive means attending to what the other is saying and doing. Nonverbal behaviors, such as making eye contact at key points when you ask a question or check your understanding (but not constantly or invasively), are useful. Gestures that are inclusive and inviting help the flow of conversation. Being sensitive to the rhythm of the other's speech and gestures and joining with it in a gentle way can help bring the two of you into harmony. Relaxed facial muscles allow you to respond in a natural way to the information that flows between you.

Sitting in a relaxed posture and inclining your head toward the other person communicates your interest. Arranging to sit kitty-corner (on the diagonal) rather than directly across from the other person indicates a conversational rather than a confrontational purpose for the discussion. Sitting or standing at the same level as the other is helpful, especially if you are seen as having legitimate power or authority over him or her by virtue of position, age, or other aspects of the relationship. For example, you will probably have a better influence conversation with a young child if you're sitting in a low chair.

The emotional and vocal tone that supports receptive behavior is relaxed, curious, and nonjudgmental. If there's an edge to your voice, the other person will probably shut down, assuming that he or she is probably in trouble with you. (If that is the case, it's better to express your point of view first, to put it on the table, or to disengage temporarily until you can use receptive behavior in a more nonjudgmental way.) Be especially careful to leave silence after you speak, to allow the other person time to think about and make a response. Don't step on his or her lines.

You shouldn't leave the other with the impression that you're not interested or have nothing to say about a topic if that's not the case. You can be alert for nonverbal signs that he or she has completed a thought or gotten to the bottom of an issue, so you will know when to interject an expressive comment. Notice, for example, when the other person drops his or her voice at the end of a sentence and adopts a more relaxed posture.

Using Receptive Influence at Work

The most obvious use of receptive influence at work is to obtain information that will help you guide others' thinking about issues. In most organizations, information is an important source of power, and significant data is not always readily available.

You can't get someone's help or shared commitment to a goal without knowing how the other person is thinking about the issue involved. You can't sell someone on an idea or proposal if you don't know his or her decision criteria. You can't negotiate a good and fair agreement with someone if you don't know what he or she wants or needs in relation to the subject at hand. You can't resolve conflicts unless you know how each party is interpreting the situation and what each feels is to be gained or lost.

- "What ideas do you have about the new exhibition booth?" (*Ask open-ended questions*)
- "So, your decision will be based primarily on whether the proposal helps us meet the customer's need for scalability." (*Check understanding*)
- "What would it take for you to commit to this schedule?" (*Pose challenging questions*)
- "If I were you, I might be worried about how this will affect my budget for next year." (*Identify with other*)

Receptive behaviors invite others to contribute and grow in confidence and skill. A young executive I once worked with had moved rather quickly from being an outstanding individual contributor to being the head of an important department. He prided himself on having excellent solutions to nearly every problem that his group had to deal with, and he shared them with his staff in the hope that they would learn from him. Yet his people were not developing in the way that he had hoped; he was growing impatient with their lack of imagination. After receiving some rather difficult feedback (as part of a coaching process), he realized that he was not in the habit of asking questions and listening to the ideas that his very talented people tentatively put forward. One day he made a memorable statement: "I'm no longer in the business of being a star; now I have to create stars." He knew that "no great idea ever entered the mind through the mouth," and so he decided to use only receptive behaviors at his next staff meeting. To his surprise and delight, his staff was full of ideas—and very excited about having the chance to express them.

One of the mistakes leaders and others often make is to accept the first response, or presenting problem, as the real issue. Thus, we spend a lot of time solving the wrong problems or trying to solve problems that others need to handle. Receptive influence behaviors allow us to learn, in depth, what the real issues are while guiding others along a path toward shared responsibility and commitment.

- "You mentioned that you were a little uncomfortable with that deadline. Tell me more about that." (*Draw out*)
- "You look as if you're uncertain whether to commit to this course of action. Is that right?" (*Test implications*)
- "Here's why I'm asking. I'm nervous about the upcoming executive committee meeting, and I want to feel totally prepared." (*Disclose*)
- "What options do you have for dealing with that problem?" (*Pose challenging questions*)

On teams, receptive influence is essential for getting members' involvement and thus their commitment and energy behind any course of action. Team members can build productive relationships quickly with one another across functional lines by using receptive influence.

- "What do you think we need to do to make this work for the customer?" (*Ask open-ended questions*)
- "Help me understand more about how you'd like me to assist with that." (*Draw out*)
- "As I understand your situation, you want to work on this with me, but your dilemma is that you don't think your functional manager would support it." (*Clarify issues*)
- "What will it take for you to be able to commit to meeting this deadline?" (*Pose challenging questions*)

In today's competitive environment, one of the keys to organizational success is the ability to learn quickly and communicate that learning to others in the organization. Organizational learning has to happen through the individual use of receptive behaviors.

- "How did you get that proposal accepted so quickly by the customer's legal department? What worked?" (*Ask open-ended questions*)
- "So, it seems that your team has gone to a shared database solution." (*Check understanding*)
- "One thing I learned on this project is that I made a big mistake in over-engineering that product; in the future I'll be more aware that the customer isn't likely to pay for that degree of perfection." (*Disclose*)

- "Like you, if it was my innovation, I'd probably want to be cautious about showing the prototype to the customer in tomorrow's meeting." (*Identify with other*)
- "You mentioned that you wouldn't use that vendor again. I'd like to hear about your experience." (*Draw out*)

Using Receptive Influence at Home

In your family or household, receptive influence helps you discover how members are feeling and involves them in decisions that will affect their lives in important ways. It's a means of expressing confidence and respect for others and, in this way, creates an atmosphere of mutual trust. Asking for and listening to others' ideas also invites them to be more open to your ideas. A very common complaint in families is, "He/she never listens to me." This is another way of saying, "I'm not respected around here. My opinions don't count."

Even young children can respond to and reciprocate with good influence behavior.

- "How do you think we should assign the housework tasks?" (*Ask open-ended questions*)
- "You've been very quiet all day. I'm wondering if you're worried about Pyewacket's visit to the veterinarian tomorrow?" (*Test implications*)
- "I shouldn't have yelled at you about breaking the dish. I know you didn't mean to do it." (*Disclose*)
- "So, you're sad that your teacher didn't choose you to go on the trip this time." (*Check understanding*)
- "What can you do to show her that you're ready for the next one?" (*Pose challenging questions*)

Children who are treated in this respectful manner are more likely to respond in a mature and productive way, regardless of age. On an outing with my then four-year-old grandson, I asked him to think about his behavior. "Isaac, why did you run away just then?"

He responded, "I forget to manage myself when I have chocolate ice cream."

"What do you think you can do about that?"

"I shouldn't ask for it."

"And what else could you do?"

"I could be the boss of me, even if I eat ice cream."

In potentially difficult or emotionally charged situations with adults and older children, it's especially important to lead with receptive behavior (using a nonjudgmental approach and tone of voice) before you find yourself in an attack-and-defend spiral. Doing this requires serious self-management, including knowing when and how to disengage if you begin to feel and act defensive.

- "Help me understand what I did that upset you just now." (*Draw out*)
- "So you waited because you expected me to pick you up as I did the last time?" (*Check understanding*)
- "If I were you, I would probably have felt angry and put down by what I said to you when I left this morning." (*Identify with other*)
- "So you were really disappointed with the way I was approaching the situation, but didn't want to embarrass me in front of the kids . . . is that right?" (*Test implications*)

Using Receptive Influence in Your Community

Many community issues bring out individuals and groups with a wide range of interests. A major task of leaders in community organizations is finding those interests that are common to all and that might hold promise of agreements or solutions. This can only be done through the judicious use of receptive behaviors.

Even large-scale meetings can be designed so that participants are invited and encouraged to listen to and learn from one another. (See the suggestions on meeting design in Appendix C.)

- "What are the issues that bring each of you to this meeting?" (*Ask open-ended questions*)
- "Do I understand you to say that no one from your group has ever been part of the leadership of this organization?" (*Check understanding*)
- "You're right. I did cut that discussion short after I promised to hear everyone's views. Let's return to it." (*Disclose*)
- "What are some things we can do that will achieve our goal without going over the budget?" (*Ask open-ended questions*)
- "In your place, I suppose I'd be reluctant to volunteer once again without a commitment from the rest of us to help you." (*Identify with other*)

Perhaps the most important use of receptive behaviors in community settings is for the purpose of understanding widely differing points of view. This is far preferable to the common situation in communities when interest groups break down into ever-smaller cohorts with single-issue themes.

When to Use Receptive Behaviors

In summary, use receptive influence behaviors at work, at home, and in your community under the following circumstances:

- You need important information that is not self-evident
- You want the other person to be committed to the decision
- You want to get to the bottom of a problem
- You need the other person to take an action that you can't take yourself
- You want to express respect for the other person and his or her opinions and ideas
- The other person has indicated, by repeating him- or herself or by withdrawing, that he or she doesn't feel listened to
- You intend to use the information that you receive in a way that the other person will agree is a benefit—or at least not harmful to him or her

Research shows that understanding how others are thinking—even more than understanding how they are feeling—can lead to better outcomes for both parties in a negotiation. Using the receptive behaviors allows us to learn about, work with, and respect both the emotional and the intellectual processes of the people we influence.

A key to successful influencing is the ability to balance expressive and receptive behaviors over time in an influence relationship. If I know that you're open to hearing my point of view, I'm much more willing to listen to yours. If I know that you're not just "picking my brain" (a graphic and unpleasant image), but are also willing to tell me what you know and think about the topic, I'll go a little further out on a limb to give you information and opinions.

CHAPTER

6

Influencing in Action

A World of Possibilities

The law of nature is, do the thing, and you shall have the power: but they who do not do the thing have not the power.

—Ralph Waldo Emerson

Responding to Opportunities

There is no shortage of influence opportunities. You're limited only by time, energy, or expectations. These opportunities come in many forms. Sometimes they occur during formal or informal meetings. Sometimes they arise spontaneously over a meal or around the coffee machine in the office. For example, someone you would like to influence may offer you opportunities such as

- A request for ideas or solutions
- A complaint about the status quo
- An expression of uncertainty or confusion
- A casual remark that touches on a subject of interest

We frequently ignore these opportunities—sometimes for good reasons and sometimes for bad reasons.

Some good reasons to turn down an opportunity to influence include

- Your experience or intuition suggests that the person is not open to influence right now.
- The issue is not important enough to you to offset the effort or the risk that you anticipate would be involved.
- The timing isn't right and you believe you would be more effective after a change in the situation (the other person's need becomes greater, you have an opportunity to get others' support, you can plan and practice an effective approach, etc.).
- You believe that you're not in a legitimate position to exercise influence on this issue with this person (for example, you might be perceived as using power because of your position or relationship; the situation calls for an expertise you do not have; etc.).

Some bad reasons to ignore an influence opportunity include

- You would prefer to settle for the status quo, even though you are uncomfortable with it, rather than risk disapproval or failure.
- You tend to keep your expectations low, rather than try to improve your chances of acquiring what you want.
- You believe that good ideas should sell themselves or that if you are in the right you should succeed without having to make a special effort.
- You're inclined to take out your frustration with the status quo by complaining or blaming others, rather than by taking action yourself.

In my family and in my company, when an issue is in contention, it's understood by everyone that the person who cares the most about something generally gets to have it his or her way—and also must shoulder the responsibility for making it happen. Influence success often carries the burden of having your name on a lot of the items on the action list—and all over the outcome. So the choice of whether or how intensely to influence about something is always tempered by how important it is to you and by how much of your resources you're willing to spend on it. That, it seems to me, is how it should be—and it gives each of us a strong motivation to succeed, if only to prove that we were right. Even the ornery side of human nature can be put to good use.

Creating Opportunities

Sometimes the right influence opportunities don't present themselves, and you have to create them. The person you need to influence may not appear at the lunch table. The issue may not arise in casual conversation. Something that is of great importance to you may not be on anyone else's screen right now. Here are some ways to create those opportunities:

- Set up a formal meeting (in person, by telephone, or electronically) on the topic and invite the people you want to be there.

- Invite the person you want to influence for lunch or coffee and raise the issue directly. This can work well for people who are more extroverts and are comfortable with thinking out loud.

- Send an e-mail or phone message indicating that you'd like to meet informally to discuss the issue. This is especially effective if the person is more introverts, someone who likes to think about a subject before discussing it.

- During a casual conversation with someone, mention that you'd like to discuss the issue with him or her. Ask whether this is a convenient time or, if not, make a date to do so.

Managing Influence Situations

The experience of managing influence situations may be a new one for you. It will require you to be thoughtful and tactical in the way you initiate and respond. In Part II of this book you'll learn how to plan and prepare for an important influence situation. Still, much of the influencing you do will be in response to opportunities that suddenly present themselves or that you're able to create in the moment. Consider the suggestions in the following list. Use them as you go about your life over the next few days. See what you can learn about influencing through some low-key experimentation. You probably won't change the world right away, but you probably won't start World War III either.

As opportunities arise, or as you can create them,

- Tell yourself what you hope will happen as a result.

  "I'd like to be assigned to that task force."

- Let the other person know what you're up to.

  "I'd like to get your ideas about how I might have more input on the project scope."

- Think about and present the situation from the other's point of view, not just your own.

  "If you can help me get the house ready, I'll be able to drive you to the mall in time to meet your friends."

- If the other person's reaction or response surprises you, use *Inquire* and/or *Listen* behaviors to understand it better.

  "So you weren't aware that I was expecting to be involved in the decision?"

- Maintain a balance of expressive and receptive behaviors. If you start by presenting an opinion or suggestion, continue by learning how the other person thinks or feels about the idea.

  "What do you think about it?" or "How does that strike you?"

- If the other person seems upset or reluctant to discuss the issue, disengage temporarily and let him or her know when you will reinitiate the discussion.

  "I can see that this isn't a good time for you to talk about this. How about if I call you early next week to set up a meeting?"

These are some ways to get started on the path of becoming conscious, tactical, and successful as an influencer. You'll continue to learn through reading, observation, conscious practice and rehearsal, feedback, experimentation, and reflection. As with any fitness program, there is no graduation (but there are continuing opportunities to test yourself).

Planning for Influence

II

Planning for Influence

Developing an Influence Plan

Design Thinking for Influence Opportunities

You think me a child of my circumstances: I make my circumstance.
—Ralph Waldo Emerson

Why Design an Influence Approach?

Design thinking is an important concept that has emerged from the fields of architecture and engineering. It's a formal method for creative problem solving when the problem is complex and multidimensional. When you follow the process of design thinking, you begin with a goal and then examine many obvious and not-so-obvious aspects of the situation before coming up with alternative and iterative solutions. You can approach an influence opportunity in a similar way. Rather than using a more rational and scientific approach where you define all parameters first, you combine analytical and intuitive methods to learn all you can about the situation. You're not looking for a "right answer" but rather for an effective approach that could lead to a variety of possible outcomes.

The Pros and Cons of Planning

Most effective influencers tend to think about and plan for influence opportunities. The good thing about planning is that you go into the situation with greater confidence because you are much clearer about where you're headed and what to anticipate along the way. This is also a bad thing about planning, because it can give you a false sense of security and may lead you to ignore things that don't happen according to your plan—or a sinking feeling when you have an excessively rigid plan and the other person isn't following it. However, if you manage yourself reasonably well, you will keep some part of your mind alert for disconfirming data. (For example, you're trying to persuade a senior person in the organization to sponsor an innovative idea and he or she seems distracted and allows interruptions to your meeting. Or your spouse, instead of being enthusiastic about your new job opportunity overseas, suggests that it might be time to try a bi-continental relationship.)

Planning can occur at many levels. At the most basic level, it means framing your influence objective before you start influencing. This is a good habit to adopt, especially when the opportunity or the need to influence arises unexpectedly. If you have time to plan more carefully, you'll want to think through the influence framework as it relates to your particular influence opportunity. And, if you have an important opportunity, you'll probably want to devise a thorough plan based on the issues you've explored. This will take time but should pay off in effectiveness and efficiency—and in achieving good results.

Just as developing your influence skills can be compared to a fitness program, planning for a specific influence situation can be compared to preparing for a journey. As in adventure travel, you need to be in shape before you start; halfway up the mountain is not the place to develop your climbing skills!

Phase One: Mapping the Territory

Each of the components of the influence framework for your opportunity contains key information that will help you succeed or at least keep you from making serious errors. In the following chapters, each component is discussed. In Appendix B, you'll find useful questions related to these areas of focus as a stimulus to your thinking. Not all of them will be relevant to your opportunity, and you may think of others that are more useful. This part of the exercise is not particularly sequential, although it helps to start with your objective. You may find as you work back and forth that you have some insights that will change your original ideas. Once you've integrated this framework into your influence approach, you'll find it a useful and quick mental exercise, even in more spontaneous situations.

Phase Two: Charting the Course

You've explored the issues in the influence framework. Now you'll decide on your approach. Here are some steps you can take in this process:

- Clarify and refine your objective.
- Highlight the most important issues related to relationship and context.
- Select the three or four most useful behaviors, using the criteria you can find in Chapter 14.
- Modify your choice of behaviors based on what you know about yourself as an influencer, as well as the fit with the culture and the individual you're influencing.
- Develop some ways of expressing what you want to say at key points, framed so you will make sense and be interesting to the other person.

Phase Three: Troubleshooting

Think about everything that could derail your plan. Do some "if...then" contingency planning. What will you do if the worst case occurs? Consider also the possibility that you may be wildly successful and may have aimed too low. How can you adjust your aspirations upward during the meeting? Think of some alternate sources of need satisfaction if this influence opportunity simply doesn't work out as you intended.

Of course, it's difficult to focus on the downside when you're trying to be optimistic. A certain amount of "magical thinking" may set in, leading you to ignore possibilities that you don't want to believe could happen. (Magical thinking is the process we use to ignore the elephant under the rug, thinking that if we don't acknowledge it, perhaps it will go away.) By remembering to take this step before you're in the situation, you'll be prepared for most eventualities and less likely to be distracted from your goal by an unexpected response. The more important the situation, the more useful it is to consider multiple possible responses and plan how to deal with the ones that will have the most impact on your results. Like the best architects or designers, you'll want to create a solid, yet flexible structure within which to work—while always considering the possibility of stepping away from your structure to rethink it.

8

Establishing Influence Objectives

What Will Success Look Like?

A good intention clothes itself with sudden power. When a god wishes to ride,
any chip or pebble will bud and shoot out winged feet, and serve him for a horse.
                                                    —Ralph Waldo Emerson

If You Don't Know Where You're Going

To paraphrase the Cheshire Cat in *Alice in Wonderland,* if you don't know where
you're going, any road will get you there. Often, the greatest distinction between
the person who comes away from a meeting with a good result and the one who is
disappointed is that the first person was clear about what he or she wanted before
the meeting began. Being aware of your objective and consciously working toward
achieving it takes time and energy but is usually considerably more effective than
improvisational advocacy. So...the first step in planning how you're going to
influence another person or group is to frame an objective.

   In this book, we'll generally use the word, "goal" to refer to the longer-term
results you hope to achieve and "objective" to mean the result you intend to

accomplish during a specific influence opportunity. Most of the time, achieving a larger goal will require that you achieve a number of influence objectives.

I've spent many difficult hours, both as a consultant and as a member of an organization, sitting in meetings and imagining what someone from another, more logical planet, might assume were the influence objectives of the participants.

Judging from the behavior used (such as sarcasm, put-downs, and direct attacks), it might seem that they were trying to do some or all of the following:

- Get a colleague to admit that he or she was bad, wrong, or stupid
- After achieving that, get the same person to acknowledge the correctness or brilliance of the influencer and/or his or her idea and to agree
- Have a third party agree with the influencer on both counts

If asked, of course, the participants would probably say that their objective was to influence the others to agree with and implement a suggestion or proposal. However, they didn't behave as if they were attempting to move the others in that direction—or else they would have noticed that everything they were doing was fixing the others more firmly in their own positions and increasing their resistance. Being clear in advance on what you hope to accomplish can help you avoid these meetings from hell and achieve the result that you really want. Making your underlying intentions conscious enables you to decide whether or not your current influence objective is one you really want to achieve.

Having a conscious goal or objective is risky; it raises common human fears of failure and of alienating others who may see us as too aggressive. If we don't make a commitment to influencing an outcome, we have the luxury of blaming others when we don't like the results of decisions that might have been within our sphere of influence. No amount of sophisticated understanding or practice of influence behaviors will make up for the reluctance to commit to an influence goal or objective. Deciding that a result is unattainable before you give it a fair shot may create short-term comfort but leads to longer-term disappointment in yourself and in your life.

You'll learn the most from this section of the book by creating an influence plan for a situation you've identified as important to your own success and well-being. In Appendix B, you'll find a template for a complete influence plan. I suggest that you try using the template, or modifying it to include issues that are important to you and exclude ones that seem irrelevant. Use it to plan for an important, upcoming influence opportunity at work, at home, or in your community. After you've implemented your plan, regardless of the outcome, make notes on what worked, what didn't, and what you learned. This is a discipline that will help you to grow and improve as an influencer. Try to make new mistakes each time, rather than repeating the same old ones. If you never make any mistakes, you're probably not taking enough risk and not doing much influencing.

Developing a Challenging Influence Objective

Your influence objective provides the motivation to succeed, so it should be attractive enough to be worth the effort, yet achievable enough to keep you from giving up too easily. I remember a high school acquaintance who attempted to prove that God did not exist by praying that the Deity would cause a light switch to fly around the room (the word "sophomoric" has useful layers of meaning in this case). Someone else remarked that he assumed any self-respecting God would have better things to do with his or her time and that he assumed the would-be atheist did also. So it is with influence goals: they should be worthy both of your time and of the efforts of the being you hope to influence.

Influence objectives must be aligned with your long-term goal and realized within a short and specific time frame. It won't help you to grow as a powerful influencer if you have to wait several weeks to see whether your behavior has achieved any results. You need to know at the time you're actively influencing whether what you're doing is moving you toward your goal. This will help you know whether and when you need to change or rethink your approach.

Your influence objective should be clear to you, not vague and amorphous. Ideally, it should be one that would be understood both by you and by the other party if you were to state it directly, using *Tell* behaviors. "I would like to influence my teammate to participate actively and contribute ideas in our team meetings" is clearer than "I would like to influence him to be a team player." Of course, you won't always begin with *Tell* behaviors, and you won't necessarily spell out your goal to the other person in so many words. However, you need to be both clear about it and focused on whether you're moving closer to it or further away.

Figure 8.1 is a useful set of criteria to test whether an influence objective will be effective. Rather than giving up on an influence result that may seem, at first, to be unattainable, use the criteria to sharpen and improve your objective. For convenience, they are summarized by the acronym, FOCUS.

- **Flexible**
- **Observable**
- **Challenging**
- **Useful**
- **Supportive**

Figure 8.1   Criteria for Influence Objectives.

Flexible

Being aware of the need that underlies your influence objective will enable you to be flexible and alert for opportunities. Through the use of receptive influence, you may become aware of alternative ways of meeting your needs that might be of more value to you or less difficult for the other person to provide. Knowing when to shift to an alternate means of need satisfaction ensures that you'll have fewer failures as an influencer. Being flexible enables you to frame your objective in a way that has a realistic chance of leading you toward success. Your influence objective should be specific enough about ends to make sure your needs are met, while being flexible enough to allow for alternative means. Specificity refers to dates, times, amounts, and so forth, and ensures that you don't settle for something that doesn't go far enough toward meeting your needs. It gives you criteria to test whether or not an alternative result can work for you. An example of an objective that is both flexible enough and specific enough might be, "To have the vestry commit today to selecting the new minister by September 30." This objective leaves room for a variety of solutions about how the selection will be made, but is firm about when.

Observable

Your influence objective should be designed so that you'll be able to observe, *during the influence opportunity*, whether you are moving closer to it or further away. This will enable you to adjust or adapt your behavior appropriately. For example, the objective, "To get my manager to change her mind about my project" is not observable. If, instead, you stated, "To get my manager to make a commitment to funding my project," you would know whether you're moving closer to or further from the result you wish to achieve.

Challenging

Your influence objective should be optimistic—possible, but a stretch—so that the effort you put forth to achieve it will seem worthwhile to you. Attempting to achieve an important influence objective always requires a degree of risk, if only of disappointing yourself, and thus is an act of courage. "I want to influence my manager to commit $10K to do an exploratory project" is more challenging than "I want to influence my manager to agree to let me spend a day working on the proposal."

Useful

We sometimes set up influence objectives that will not meet our most important needs. For example, "To have my spouse admit that he or she was wrong about the old contractor" would not be as useful as an objective that states, "To get my spouse's commitment to hire the new contractor I have found." It's helpful to question yourself about whether your influence objectives meet short-term ego needs (which almost always will have a negative impact on the influence relationship) or will lead to longer-term, more important results. Of course, there are times when meeting the shorter-term need might really be more important to you, but with the recognition that you may go down with the ship you just sank. (A former husband used to ask me, "Do you want to be right, or do you want to get the result you want?" Sometimes I had to think about it for quite a while. . . .) Make sure your objectives are not only useful but also optimistic enough to be worth pursuing.

Supportive
Although influence objectives are short-term, they need to be aligned with longer-term strategic goals in order to be effective. If you align your influence objectives with the larger goal you hope to achieve, you'll avoid being at cross-purposes with yourself, your organization, or your family and thus minimize resistance to your idea or suggestion. For example, if your long-term goal is to work abroad, you'll want to make sure that you don't set an influence objective for your manager to assign you to a long-lasting project that will keep you close to the home office.

Testing your objective statement against some or all of these criteria will lead you to sharpen and improve it so that it becomes a powerful tool for influencing. An influence objective that meets these criteria can be ambitious and optimistic, yet realistic and attainable.

The Value of Persistence

Something that clearly distinguishes successful influencers and leaders from others is that they are persistent in the pursuit of their influence goals and objectives. They don't take "no" for an answer very easily. They tend to know when to back off (see Chapter 20) and wait for another opportunity and are sensitive to when they should change their approach and tactics and try again.

Persistence helps in several ways. First of all, you may have been mistaken or were missing some important data in your original analysis of the framework for influence. Or the individual, organizational, or external context at the time wasn't supportive. Your original timing could have been off. Since then, some players may have changed, priorities may have shifted, unanticipated events may have made the picture more favorable. Perhaps your influence relationship with the other person has improved—or you could cause it to improve. Giving up too easily doesn't allow you to explore these possibilities.

Secondly, the fact that you're persistent (without being inappropriately aggressive) lends power to your influence attempts. Caring about an issue deeply enough to continue to bring it to others' attention demonstrates the strength of your commitment. One member of my staff used to greet me with a cheerful, "I'm baaaack!" before he launched into another pitch for something he believed to be important. He knew that eventually his persistence would pay off, although he might have had to be flexible about his approach and about specifics such as timing and cost. He would often make several strategic retreats and try again before I was sufficiently worn down to agree—but his success rate was high, and I was not put off by his efforts.

CHAPTER

9

Focus on the Relationship

Influence Works Both Ways

Let us be poised, and wise, and our own, today. Let us treat the men and women well: treat them as if they were real; perhaps they are.

—Ralph Waldo Emerson

You, Me, and Us

During a previous marriage that was marked by an excessive amount of navel-gazing (from my point of view), I remember saying in exasperation, "It seems that there are always three of us to deal with here . . . you, me, and the relationship." In fact, we are different in each of our personal, business, and other influence relationships. Each of us has aspects of our culture, personality, talents, education, experience, associations, interests, and memories that connect in different ways with different people. In this way, each relationship is unique. Each person knows and connects to some aspects of me that would surprise another person. One friend sees me as goal-directed and organized; another experiences me as a flake. One direct report finds my lack of attention to detail rather charming, making room for her to grow, while another is constantly disappointed that I need a reminder from him if he wants my input by a specific date. I have a very different influence relationship with each of them.

Influence relationships don't have to be very close; you don't even have to like one another. But you do need to acknowledge that there is a value to the relationship, that mutual respect and support is important, that "one hand washes the other." You need to know that you can trust the other person to keep agreements, to respect confidentiality, to approach the relationship with the intention of being fair. You need to believe that you have enough vested interests in common that you will both want to maintain the balance in the relationship.

The content of the influence message is filtered through what we believe or perceive about the relationship. This frequently determines how likely we are to be influenced by this person on this topic at this time. Understanding what makes a particular influence relationship unique will help make it successful. Knowing what values and goals you share, what the other trusts you to know about, and what is likely to create conflict means that you will less often be surprised or unprepared to influence (or be influenced by) this particular person.

The Importance of Balance

Overall, the most important thing to remember about influence relationships is that they only work well when they're kept in balance most of the time. That means that neither party feels that he or she is always the target, rather than the initiator of influence. Both parties should have relatively equal expectations of gaining support from or influencing the decisions of the other.

One way to ensure that this is so is to make sure that you use both expressive and receptive behaviors whenever you influence, so there will always be an opening for the other to respond and to shape the outcome. Another way is to have regular check-ins with the people who are the most important to your success. You can do this in a low-key way and be quite explicit with one another about what is working and what needs to change in your influence relationship. But it only works if you check in on a regular basis—not just when a relationship crisis looms.

Studying History versus Being Condemned to Repeat It

Sometimes you choose the people with whom you will have an important influence relationship; often they choose you or are chosen for you. In all cases, it's important to remember that the past creates the future. Before you begin to influence in a new relationship, find out something about what the person might be expecting from you. These expectations might be based on past history with your organization, profession, or department, other people in your role, or past experiences with you that you may not recall (or with someone like you). Using receptive behavior to learn about preferred norms or processes (how he or she would like to work together on this), as well as any concerns or preferences he or she might have, can get the relationship off to a good start.

If you're surprised by the other person's reaction to your influence behavior, stop the process and ask about it or, if that is inappropriate, disengage temporarily and ask someone who is in a position to know what the problem might be. If you learn about a past problem that might be creating concern or wariness in the present, avoid any tendency to become defensive or to try to justify previous actions or behavior. Instead, use this as a learning opportunity. Use receptive behavior to find out all you can about it. If necessary, disclose and acknowledge your part in or your organization's contribution to any issues that may be affecting the current influence opportunity. Use expressive behavior to let the other person know where you stand now and what you hope to achieve by working together.

Creating Your Influence Future

Each time you influence someone, you're making it easier or more difficult to influence him or her in the future. A successful and balanced outcome will motivate both of you to repeat the process, building a longer-term and more effective relationship.

If you plan to be part of an organization, industry, or profession for the long run, there's no time like the present to build new and strong influence relationships. The very person you write off or treat disrespectfully today may be in a position to give or withhold support for something important to you tomorrow.

Some ways you can build influence relationships for the future include

- Fix anything that is broken in a current influence relationship, and do it at a time when you're not seeking to influence that person.
- Seek out people with interesting ideas and learn more about them.
- Ask people you respect but don't know well to help you on a task or project.
- Offer to help someone whom you would like to get to know better on a task or project.
- Give public credit to people whose ideas you like and use.
- Invite a new person to join a task force or participate in a "think tank" meeting.
- Take time to congratulate a coworker on a job well done.

Over time, your influence relationships will become a rich source of ideas, information, referrals, and mutual support. These people will be your coalition partners, champion your ideas, recommend you for that promotion, write blurbs for the cover of your book, hire your children as summer interns, and stand up and be counted when you need them. You don't have to take them out to dinner, but it wouldn't hurt to do lunch once in a while.

CHAPTER

10

Focus on the Context

The Individual

All persons are puzzles until at last we find in some word or act the key to the man, to the woman; straightway all their past words and actions lie in light before us.

—Ralph Waldo Emerson

Influence Happens in the Other Person

Annoying, but there it is. No matter how well you have convinced yourself that your idea is the best thing since postable notes, if the other person doesn't buy it, you haven't influenced. It would be a perfect (albeit boring) world if everyone thought like you do; since they don't, you have to know as much as possible about the person you need to influence.

I once had a client who was the senior vice president of engineering in a large public utility. He was working on being more effective with the executive committee. I asked him to tell me how he usually approached them when he wanted funding for a project. He explained how carefully he put together the proposals with an emphasis on important structural engineering details as well as costs. Unfortunately for him, nearly all the members of the executive committee were attorneys and were primarily interested in safety issues and what their exposure might be to lawsuits. The details of the design were not reassuring to them. They were not impressed with, and thus not influenced by, his proposals because their questions and concerns were not addressed. It was a big "aha" for him to realize that he should find out what their decision criteria were and let them be his guide, rather than share data that was convincing to him.

Understanding Values, Needs, and Aspirations

Three important things to understand about the person you wish to influence (and about yourself) in relation to your influence objective are

1. *Values*: What does he or she believe should happen?
2. *Needs*: What does he or she need or want to happen?
3. *Aspirations*: What does he or she hope will happen?

Values usually come from one's culture, family, or profession. They are beliefs about what is right, true, and good; we use them as the basis for important decisions. An example would be, "I believe that everyone should be consulted on issues that will affect them directly." Needs have to do with current vested interests—what she or he has to gain or lose related to the issue at hand. An example is, "I need to have input on the reorganization of my project team." The third question has to do with longer-term aspirations, hopes, and dreams; for example, "I want to be involved in this decision in order to gain valuable leadership experience that will help me grow in my career."

An important influence issue may involve any or all of these. Some issues are more value-based ("What should be included in our code of conduct?"). Some stimulate questions of vested interests ("Which project will we fund, and who will lead it?"). Some are related to important aspirations ("Where should I go to school?").

Suppose, for example, that you want to persuade your neighbor to help you initiate a community garden project. On the one hand, he or she may value the idea of neighborhood cooperation, or on the other hand, be a strong proponent of individual family privacy. Perhaps your neighbor has a strong need for a say in neighborhood aesthetic decisions—or perhaps he or she has a demanding job and needs weekends and evenings to be available to his or her family. Does he or she hope to be a community leader or aspire to move to a more upscale neighborhood? Understanding the values, needs, and aspirations of your neighbor can help you choose a realistic, wise approach to influencing him or her on this issue.

Understanding values, needs, and aspirations can, in some cases, lead you to modify your objective or decide to seek support elsewhere.

To learn a great deal about another person's values, needs, and aspirations, you only need to look and listen. Look at what is on display in his or her office or private space. Listen to the words, phrases, and themes that are emphasized over and over again in casual conversation and in meetings. Pay attention to what the person responds to favorably and his or her "hot buttons." You need not be secretive about it—we all like to discuss these things and usually prefer that the people we live and work with closely understand and respect our preferences.

It's essential to know that you can't change anyone's values, needs, or aspirations through direct influence. You can expose others to alternative options and ideas, but you will have to stay out of their way while they deal with any internal changes they might choose to make. (This is particularly difficult when we are influencing family members or friends.) You can, however, keep their values, needs, and aspirations in mind as you influence them to take certain actions. If you can find an honest way to frame what you want them to do that is consonant with their values, needs, or aspirations, most of your work will be done for you. And you will have treated the person with respect. For example, a school counselor I once knew wanted to influence her principal not to suspend a boy with whom she was working. The child had gradually improved his behavior during the year as a result of a lot of hard work on her part, as well as his. She believed that, with a sustained effort, he would turn around, and that a suspension would interrupt the progress that was being made, especially because attendance was an issue for him. That morning, however, he had disrupted a class and the principal wanted to teach him a lesson. The principal was an ex-military officer who believed in a strictly enforced disciplinary code. The counselor knew that approaching him with a plea for leniency or anything he might read as excusing the boy's behavior would be useless. Instead, she stated, "I know how important it is to you that children be held responsible for their actions. I believe that we should not give him the 'out' of suspending him but rather insist that he deal directly with the teacher and make an agreement with her to do something that will make up for the problems he caused." This was a realistic and honest alternative way of assessing the situation and presenting the case. It made good sense from the point of view of the principal. He accepted the suggestion.

If you understand these fundamentals, you can think your way into the other's mind and predict how he or she might respond to a specific influence issue. This will help you to prepare. For example, you can show him how the action you are hoping to stimulate will fit within his values. You can demonstrate to her how doing this will meet her needs. You can show how your aspirations are aligned around this issue. This is often called "reframing," and it is a powerful technique (see Chapter 14).

Working with Personality, Interests, and Preferences

There are many ways of classifying personality and preference. Some of them are well-researched, self-report instruments, such as the Myers-Briggs Type Indicator; some are based on feedback, and others depend more on your own intuition and observation. Anything that helps you understand which approaches usually work well or usually fail with a specific person will contribute to your success as an influencer. If you always approach other people in the way you prefer to be approached, you will likely be successful primarily with those who are most like you. This is a limitation most of us don't have the luxury of accepting.

Although it may seem surprising, most people are more than happy to let you know how to be successful in influencing them. In our *Exercising Influence*™ seminar, participants bring to class with them assessments from five or six colleagues. Although some participants express concern because the forms are not anonymous (because influence is very specific to particular relationships, anonymous feedback would not be very useful), few people have trouble getting important people in their lives to fill them out. Many people welcome the opportunity to tell their managers, peers, or key subordinates how to be more successful in influencing them! Participants often ask someone from their households or friends to fill one out as well. They are instructed to follow up in a way that will enable them to discuss in an open and productive way what the other would like them to do more of, less of, or differently.

In Appendix F, there is a short version of this assessment. You can fill it out on yourself, ask someone else to do it, or imagine what someone you need to influence might tell you about what you could do more of, less of, or differently. Once someone has let you know what works best, there is a certain tendency for him or her to show you that the recommended approach works. This can contribute significantly to your success, to both persons' benefit.

All of this will help when you come to choose the influence behaviors that will be the best tools for achieving your objective with this person. Once you understand what works well with someone, you don't have to use only that behavior. It may not be the right tool for the job you have to do. But you might want to use that behavior to set yourself up for success, to create rapport or a comfort zone between you and the other person. For example, with someone who values your friendship and is open in expressing feelings, you might want to begin influencing with an honest disclosure. "Sam, I'm uncomfortable in asking you to do one more thing on this project. I've had to come to you so many times in the past month." With someone who is more analytical, you could begin with a summary of why you need him or her to help you. In both cases, you will probably use *Negotiate* behaviors to do the real influence work, but you opened the discussion by using an approach that respects the other person's preferences. In addition, you'll probably avoid using a behavior that drives the other person up the wall (yes, some people are allergic to your beautifully crafted rationales . . . or visions . . . or questions) and use one that will do the job almost as well.

It's always useful to keep in mind any vested interests that the other may have. Be sure you're not asking the other to go against those interests, and, if you can, find a way to align your interests with those of the other person. See whether you can meet some need in a way that is legitimate and fair, given what you're asking of him or her. Seek to understand any problems that might be created if the person does what you ask, and find a way to make it easier for him or her to say "yes." Finding common ground between you and the other person—something you both have to gain by your success—is often a key prerequisite to successful influencing in difficult situations. For example, "I know I'm asking a lot of you and your team by moving up the deadline. I'd be willing to assign a couple of additional engineers to your project to help speed things along."

Examining Your Assumptions

Most of what we think we know about other people is not tested. We see or hear something they say or do and immediately explain it to ourselves. We categorize it (limited, of course, by our previous experience or the book we just finished). If someone is important for you to influence, try noticing how you are explaining that person to yourself. ("She didn't stop by my desk this morning. She must be angry with me. Or maybe she noticed that I didn't include her in the conference invitation." "He's a sales guy; he won't want a detailed report.") Then, during the next few times you see that person, just notice what he or she does without making assumptions. Consider a variety of alternate explanations that fit the same facts. Then, before you have an important influence opportunity with this person, use your receptive behavior to learn something new about him or her. Find out, for example, how she or he likes to go about making decisions; what kind of information is helpful; how the person prefers to be influenced.

Assumptions make life easier; they also limit our freedom to experiment. Untested assumptions about the person we intend to influence can lead us down a fruitless path. We keep waiting for the person to behave in the expected way. When he or she doesn't, we become confused or angry. Or we avoid opportunities to influence, assuming that the other will not be open to change. A more constructive approach is to notice and question your assumptions about the person. Say, "What would I do if I didn't believe that?" Then do it.

Difficult People or Difficult Situations?

You've tried everything. You've been rational. You've been sensitive. You've been generous. You've been tough. Nothing has worked. Where, you ask, is the section on dealing with difficult people?

There isn't one. There isn't room for one. Because everyone is difficult for somebody, sometimes. Even you. Saying that someone is too difficult to deal with means saying you've given up on influencing that person. Of course, you might want to do that... but if the issue is important enough, you won't. Instead, you will do your homework, find someone who can help you understand this person, examine your assumptions, try a different approach, do something that seems completely insane, vary your timing, or use some indirect influence.

And if that doesn't work, take the day off, and then figure out another way to get what you need. As George Herbert said in 1670 or so, "Living well is the best revenge." (I know, I always thought it was Dorothy Parker, too.)

CHAPTER 11

Focus on the Context

System, Organization, Culture, and Timing

Every moment instructs, and every object: for wisdom is infused into every form.
—Ralph Waldo Emerson

Influencing in an Open System

It's all very well to know everything you can about the person you're going to influence and the issue you're going to influence about. You can even be exceptionally good at the influence behaviors you have decided to use and still end up without the result you hoped for—or with one that makes your worst-case scenario look like a tea party.

Often that is because you've left a few important things out of your analysis, and they turned out to be the most important ingredients. It's as if your great-aunt Jane gave you the recipe for her famous chocolate cake, but just happened to leave out one or two items, and the cake turned out flat and tasted like chalk.

The reason that so many good influence intentions come to naught is that you're almost never dealing with a tabula rasa—a blank slate—a situation completely divorced from other realities. The slate has been written on. Every influence opportunity is part of a larger, open system that involves a variety of other issues, people, organizations, cultures, and other things, tangible or intangible, that exist in or out of time and space. Any one of them can override your best plans or make your needs irrelevant. An "open system" is one that receives information from outside of itself (inputs), transforms it, and sends information back out (outputs). This is a good description of the organizations we work in and the families we are a part of. Many of the elements that enter an open system are outside of your sphere of influence but should affect the way you choose to approach the influence opportunity. For example, you may wish to influence a senior manager to make a commitment to an important project. You've planned your approach for some time and have aligned it with the strategic business goals of the company. Now you've learned that a large firm from another country has acquired the company. You must assume that the strategic business goals have changed. This will affect the way you approach the manager.

Because you're not going to be able to control, influence, or even know about all the important inputs to the system, the only defense is to ask yourself a few questions about absolutely anything that could derail or, for that matter, enhance your attempt to influence. You need to begin by scanning the system for what could cause problems or help you, and then "debug" or adjust your approach to take these issues into account. Usually you'll find that there are some current and compelling issues related to the person you are trying to influence, such as competing priorities and deadlines. Maybe there are other people who are important to the person's decision and who have an issue with you or your idea. There may be organizational "hot buttons" (words, concepts, or ideas that stimulate a strong reaction because of historical or other associations), major initiatives, or competitive pressures. There may be some industry or cultural imperatives that you can't ignore. And, of course, there may be trends and issues in the world surrounding the system that can promote or prevent your idea from receiving a fair hearing at this time.

In Appendix B, you'll find a list of questions that will help you explore the system you're working within so that you can take advantage of opportunities or deal with problems as part of your influence planning process. By using them, you can create a better fit between your idea or proposal and the system within which you are influencing.

Organizations, Teams, and Families

Every human organization has its own current issues and priorities, its own way of operating, its own structure and politics. For example, in my family of origin, issues that were emotional were dealt with when my father was out of town; he was very uncomfortable with conflict. My brother and I soon learned that if we brought up a contentious issue (that he and I agreed about) when Dad was around, we would often end up with a better deal from our more peace-loving parent than if we left it for our mother to settle with us. Knowing how the power structure works is useful. Equally important is an understanding of current strategy, goals, and priorities. It's far easier to sell an idea that is aligned with those goals and priorities than one that is tangential, unrelated, or pulling in a different direction.

To develop a better fit between your idea and the organization, focus first on where the organization is expending the most energy. If you can communicate how your idea solves a key organizational problem, supports important priorities, or speeds the way to achieving an important goal, you have a much better chance of success. Next, review the organization's structures and processes to make sure that you develop an approach that aligns with the way the organization (or team, or family) works. Study the norms or ground rules that suggest who to approach, and how and when to approach him or her. For example, my company sells training and development services. In some organizations, we are more successful when we deal with senior leaders directly. In others, we enter through the human resources or organization development groups, because they are in a strategic role and, as our colleagues, want to be in the loop.

Culture Is Context

Just as we assume that the fish has no concept of water, we seldom think about culture. It's just there—unless, of course, we find ourselves in one that's different from our own. And even then it takes work to realize that the Italians are not driving like that just to annoy you and the Japanese are not deliberately dragging out the preliminaries to the negotiation in order to wear you down. Culture can be national, regional, ethnic, or organizational. Professions and industries have cultures; even families, departments, and teams develop a set of norms, values, rituals, myths, and taboos that can be seen as cultural. Cultural practices drive a great deal of behavior that is below our awareness and easy for others to misinterpret.

The ability to recognize when behavior is cultural rather than tactical (deliberately chosen to achieve a goal) is very useful to the influencer in reading the situation. Understanding the cultural context also helps you shape your influence approach in a way that will be a better fit for the person or group you're influencing. For example, the culture of a research and development organization is likely to be one in which expertise and reputation are highly valued. You would be well-advised to brush up on your chemistry or physics or (preferably) bring along someone whom the other person respects professionally if your influence opportunity involves anything remotely technical.

Timing Is Everything—Almost

Knowing what to do is one thing, and knowing when to do it is another. Once we've decided to take on an influence task and have prepared for it, it can be difficult to stop and wait. But timing has to be part of your recipe for success. There are times when moving on something quickly before the other person has too many options to deal with is the right thing to do. Sometimes it makes sense to wait until there are fewer demands on his or her attention or for a time when the issue is on his or her screen. Often, you'll want to carry out your plan in stages. Nothing works all the time, but a well-thought-out plan considers timing as well as approach.

12

Focus on the Context

Yourself

Insist on yourself; never imitate.

—Ralph Waldo Emerson

Wants versus Needs

At its core, influence is about getting what you want. Even though what you want may be to save the world or at least some small part of it, your influence goal or specific objective is still more about you than about the world. So it's best to be very upfront with yourself about what it is that you want and what underlying needs or vested interests getting it would serve. A simple way to do that is to revisit your goal and ask yourself what it represents for you. Asking, "What would achieving this goal do for me?" is a simple way to get at your own motivations for influence. Sometimes by doing so we're clarified and strengthened in our commitment. Sometimes we realize that it's all about ego gratification and, in fact, a facelift or a new sports car would be cheaper. If you're not completely honest with yourself, you could find that getting what you tell yourself you want will not satisfy your underlying need. Honesty with yourself also has the bracing effect of helping you modify unrealistic influence goals or objectives, such as making your teenager admit that you are right about his or her hair. (Influencing him or her to change the hairdo would be a more realistic objective.)

Strengths and Limitations

Having made a tentative commitment to go ahead and influence, you might as well review how hard you'll have to work at it. If you've decided to do something that plays to your strengths (expertise, behavioral skill, reputation, comfort in a relationship), you will probably go ahead right away (if the timing is right). If not—if you have to work with a person with whom you have had tremendous conflict, or use a behavior that's very difficult for you to do with a straight face, or speak knowledgeably about a subject that you nearly flunked in elementary school—consider your options. Perhaps you need more time to prepare and a friend to rehearse with. Maybe you need to find someone to go with you or instead of you (see Chapter 20 on indirect influence). Perhaps you just need to alter your plan off the ideal course enough so that it fits you better.

Style and Blind Spots

Knowing yourself as an influencer can sometimes keep you out of trouble. Do you prefer or need time to think before you speak, or do you do best when you can respond in the moment? Do you like a lot of structure and preparation, or do you prefer a more spontaneous approach? Do you enjoy taking risks by suggesting new ideas, or do you prefer to come in with a well-documented case? Do you enjoy David and Goliath moments (where you play David), or do you try to gain a balance of power before you go in?

Knowing what you prefer as an influencer doesn't mean that you can—or should—do it your way. In fact, understanding it may keep you from doing it your default way when that style would not be appropriate to the situation. Comfort is not one of the common components of influencing. You need to be wide awake and manage yourself. Blind spots are only blinding when you keep yourself unaware of them.

Think about any personal issues you have that are specific to this situation. Are you carrying any baggage about this person that could get in the way of being an effective influencer? Do you have any unfinished business or hidden agenda that you are aware of? If so, think of a way to settle it or set it aside before this influence opportunity. It will interfere with your effectiveness.

Keeping It Light

Nothing will drag you down as an influencer more than your awareness of the heaviness of your responsibility and the serious nature of what you are taking on. The natural fear of failure that we all have will expand, like any clutter, to fit the space available to it. The more important the influence attempt, and the more seriously you take yourself as an influencer, the more likely you are to slip on a banana peel, like the policemen in old silent films. There is a paradox about this business of influence. When we treat it as a sort of "theater game" of skill and chance, where we can move forward and back and sideways and up and down, and maybe have the other players get tangled up in unpredictable ways, we may prevail. When we treat it as a life-and-death drama starring ourselves as the heroes—well, after all those hours spent just in putting on the makeup, it's hard to improvise. Influence is nothing if not improvisational theater. Keep some corner of your mind available to be amused at your own antics, and you will always have enough objectivity to allow yourself to take advantage of subtle shifts in the situation.

Readiness, Reluctance, and Risk

Influencing takes energy. (It can also be very energizing.) You need to decide which goals are worth your effort. Sometimes you will influence to achieve a goal that's personally meaningful to you. Sometimes others will ask or tell you to be influential about something that you don't care about very much—or even something you don't agree with. Sometimes you'll be daunted by an important or difficult influence opportunity. Sometimes the opportunity may seem too trivial to bother with. Knowing yourself as an influencer requires you to be ruthlessly honest about your commitment to achieving a long-term influence goal. If you're not committed, you're unlikely to succeed. Most influence goals that are really worth achieving require some risk taking on the part of the influencer. You will have to take a stand about something that may be unusual, innovative—even unpopular. You may need to communicate with people who have more power than you do or who have the ability to influence your career or your personal well-being, for good or ill. You may be a person who prefers to avoid conflict and controversy. Influential people are visible, and the attention you attract may not always be to your liking. Balancing the strength of your commitment with the level of risk you're willing to take to achieve your goal will give you a realistic sense of your readiness to respond to an influence opportunity. If the risk seems too high, you can explore indirect influence options, take other steps to reduce the risk level, or let go of the goal. Any of those options is preferable to making a halfhearted attempt to influence. You won't get the results you want, and you will probably reduce your effectiveness and confidence as an influencer.

Focus on the Issues

What's at Stake?

A foolish consistency is the hobgoblin of little minds.

—Ralph Waldo Emerson

Doing Your Homework

That's it, basically. If you have something important to influence about, learn everything you can about it. Read everything you can find, talk to everyone who knows more about it than you do. Don't limit yourself by looking only for support or justification of your point of view. Get familiar with all the counterarguments and all the potential threats that are related to your idea—all the needs and fears that might arise for someone who actually had to agree to take action on it. Put yourself in the place of the person you wish to influence and make an educated guess about the specific issues that your request or offer will raise for her or him. Think yourself into the mind of someone who would be unalterably opposed to doing what you want done and then see what it would take to change your mind, even to warm up to the idea just a little.

Develop a list of benefits and costs for taking action—not just for you (although that will be useful), but for the person or group you hope to influence. Do a risk analysis. Identify what could go wrong and how such problems could be prevented or mitigated. Be sure to do this from your target person's point of view. Think about the risks of not taking action at all.

Anything you can do to stimulate dissatisfaction with the status quo may help move your idea forward. Some ways to do that include

- Showing objective data that indicates problems with the current approach (decreasing sales figures, plunging grades, etc.)
- Providing information from third parties about needs or problems with the current situation (letters from neighbors, customer complaints, etc.)
- Finding benchmark examples of successful implementation of an idea or approach similar to the one you support
- Planning an evaluation with the group, team, or family to test what is and is not working about the present situation

Influencing people generally means getting them to change or modify the way they think, feel, or act. Behavioral scientists, such as the late Richard Beckhard of the Sloan School of Management at MIT, have suggested that change occurs under the following conditions. There is

- sufficient dissatisfaction with the present state, and
- a positive vision of a future possibility, and
- support for getting from the present to the ideal future state.

Each of these must exist in sufficient strength to balance the perceived risks of change. The information you gather about the issue can serve to strengthen the other person's understanding in any of these areas.

When you have gathered the information, consider how best to present it to the person you want to influence. This kind of information is often most effective when the other person has a chance to absorb it on his or her own before you discuss it. You'll also want to think about choosing information that focuses on the merits of your idea, rather than criticizing the status quo or viewpoint of the person you want to influence. It's best if you let the other person do that. It is easier to get someone to think about your idea as another, more useful alternative than to escape unscathed from someone who is fiercely defending his or her previous choices and decisions.

Even with all the homework you are doing, it's possible that you'll persuade someone to agree that the situation needs to change, without deciding that your preferred solution or idea is the way to go. Consider possible alternatives and how close they would come to meeting your need or achieving your goal. You may even have to shift to a slightly different "ideal result" if it looks as if you won't achieve your original goal. Having already considered alternatives gives you some useful flexibility.

Framing the Issue

The way an issue or suggestion is framed can make all the difference in how another person receives it. Framing is the process of presenting an issue or idea so that the listener interprets it in a particular manner. Jim Kuypers, an academic specializing in communication, suggests that frames operate in four ways: defining problems, diagnosing causes, making moral judgments, and suggesting remedies.* With influence, we're especially interested in the latter function—framing ideas or solutions to problems by increasing the urgency, importance, or priority for specific issues or concerns, and getting others to agree to a particular plan of action or to take a certain role or responsibility.

There are usually many possible ways to frame an issue. You may have selected one frame that is meaningful to you, but other ways of looking at it may be equally legitimate. As discussed in Chapter 10, understanding the other person's values, goals, and vested interests or the organization's strategic priorities can help you frame the issue you're influencing about in a way that appeals to that person or organization. Connecting a new idea to one that's accepted as received wisdom can be useful.

Confidence Is Power

The best thing about doing your homework is that it gives you confidence. Confidence that you know what you are talking about. Confidence that you're prepared to deal with questions and objections. Confidence has a very attractive quality: It lets the other person know that he or she can trust you on the issue. That is, unless you use your confidence in a manipulative way, by asking "trap questions" or otherwise putting down the other's position. Having confidence enables you to build up your position without tearing down that of the other. That way, you won't have to deal with defensive and self-protective resistance to your ideas.

---

*Adapted from J. Kuypers' 2009 book, *Rhetorical Criticism: Perspectives in Action.*

Choosing and Using Influence Behaviors to Achieve Your Objective

How to Create Your Approach

A beautiful behavior is better than a beautiful form: it gives a higher pleasure than statues or pictures; it is the finest of the fine arts.

—Ralph Waldo Emerson

Reviewing the Influence Framework

During the preliminary influence planning process, you have established your objective and thought about the person you're influencing and your influence relationship. You've explored other factors in the context into which you'll be influencing. All of this information will help you choose your tactics—the behaviors you'll consciously choose and use to move toward the result you want to accomplish—that will help you achieve your objective.

Look over the notes you've made and highlight the things that seem especially significant to this influence opportunity. In general, the more important the influence opportunity, the more elements you'll take the time to consider. Now you're ready to develop a plan of action.

Selecting the Most Useful Behaviors

Tables 14.1 and 14.2 show criteria for selecting behaviors that will be most effective in your situation. You've probably already made a preliminary choice. In many cases, you'll simply confirm this. However, the criteria will enable you to notice where context issues could make a particular behavior less effective than you would like. In that case, you can either select another behavior or, if there really is no practical alternative, you can do something to change the context. For example, if the situation requires that you make a suggestion about something where the other doesn't consider you an expert, you'll probably want to enlist a person who is respected in that field to work with you.

In addition, you'll want to use your ability to identify with the other person to imagine what specific issues might arise once your suggestion, request, or offer is on the table. Once you can articulate several possible issues, your choice of behaviors may become clear. For example, you ask your manager to provide you with additional resources for your project. Some issues that may come up for her include

- Where will I find an additional resource?
- Will others see that as unfair?
- How can I justify that to my manager?
- What difference will that resource make to the project's success?

With these concerns in mind, you will probably think about using *Inquire* (to go deeper into understanding her concerns), *Tell* (to express your need or make a suggestion), *Negotiate* (to offer an exchange that would make her decision seem more fair), and perhaps *Enlist* (to communicate a vision of the desired result). Using Tables 14.1 and 14.2, you can consider which of the behaviors in each tactic might be most useful. Of course, there's never a "school solution" for the best influence approach—there are too many variables. Still, this process can help you to work out a "draft plan" for your opportunity.

Once you've decided on three or four behaviors, use the "sentence starters" in Appendix D to develop some ways to use them. You won't be reading from a script during the real event, but this practice will enable you to become more comfortable with the behaviors, especially if they're not the ones you use most often.

Table 14.1   Guidelines for Choosing Expressive Behaviors.

Use *Tell* behaviors when	Use *Sell* behaviors when
• The other is uncommitted on the issue.	• The issue is open to different ideas, solutions, and interpretations.
• You have a clear direction you want to take.	• You can be relatively objective.
• Choose *Suggest* when the other has defined the issue as a problem and you are seen as an expert.	• Choose *Offer reasons* when you are seen as an expert on the issue.
• Choose *Express needs* when the other would see your need as legitimate.	• Choose *Refer to goals and benefits* when you are seen as a partner.
• *Do not use* if the action would be against the other's interests.	• *Do not use* if you are not open to influence on the issue.

Use *Negotiate* behaviors when	Use *Enlist* behaviors when
• Vested interest are involved.	• You are on the same "team."
• The other perceives you as fair.	• The other is hesitant to take action.
• Choose *Offer incentives* when you have tangible or intangible resources to exchange.	• Choose *Encourage* when the other respects you and you are willing to offer help and support.
• Choose *Describe consequences* when the other needs to know about them in order to make a good choice.	• Choose *Envision* when you want to align and motivate.
• *Do not use* if you are unwilling to deliver on them.	• *Do not use* if you are not genuinely enthusiastic.

Reframing

In the previous chapter, we introduced the concept of framing—how you conceptualize and present ideas, requests, or solutions. One of the most important preparations for a specific influence opportunity is to use what you know about the other person to *reframe* your ideas in a way that will make sense within his

Table 14.2   Guidelines for Choosing Receptive Behaviors.

Use *Inquire* behaviors when

- The other wants to be consulted or involved.
- You are genuinely interested in what he or she has to say.

- Choose Ask **Open-ended questions** when you are opening a new topic.
- Choose **Draw out** when you want to go deeper.
- **Do not use** if the other does not trust you.

Use *Listen* behaviors when

- The other believes you have a right to know.
- The other believes you can identify with his/her concerns.

- Choose **Check understanding** when the information is relatively straightforward.
- Choose **Test implications** when you want to deepen your understanding.
- **Do not use** if you feel hostile toward the other.

Use *Attune* behaviors when

- You would like to create more openness.
- The other has a need for allies.

- Choose **Identify with other** when the other already trusts you.
- Choose **Disclose** when you are willing to make yourself somewhat vulnerable in exchange for more openness.
- **Do not use** if you don't trust how the other would use the information.

Use *Facilitate* behaviors when

- The other is accountable for taking action.
- The other would not lose face by accepting assistance from you.

- Choose **Clarify issues** when the other seems to be "stuck."
- Choose **Pose challenging questions** when the other needs a stimulus toward action.
- **Do not use** if you have a specific action in mind.

or her model of the world. Earlier, we discussed the importance of understanding the values, needs, and aspirations of the other. Once you do, you're in a position to take an idea that's important to you and frame it so that the other person can understand and see the value of it. This doesn't mean being dishonest; there are usually many different ways of looking at the same set of data.

You'll need to look at the issue through the other person's frame if you are to be influential. For example, as a parent, you may want to influence your child's teacher to provide more individual attention and challenging assignments, rather than punishing him for misbehavior that you know comes from boredom. You know that she wants to be seen as a supportive and helpful person. Rather than telling her what you think she is doing wrong, you might mention how much pleasure your son received from the time she spent with him, working on a special art project (*Encourage*).

Planning Your Approach

The most useful parts of your approach to plan in some detail are

- The first few minutes of the meeting or conversation: How will you start?
- Key transition points: How will you introduce or handle difficult issues?
- Conclusion: How will you move toward closure?

Remember, this will not be a play in which you and the other person have blocked the action and rehearsed your lines. It will be improvisational theater, and things will happen that you don't expect. If you prepare for that possibility in your planning, you can anticipate and respond to these events. So—put some "what-ifs" in your plan. Troubleshoot it. Think about the worst case and what you might do if it happens. Think about what might be a signal that things are going off course. Then decide what to do if this should occur. For example, what if your influence target becomes angry? What if he or she presents you with a major piece of information that is a complete surprise? Consider what could trigger a decision to set your objective aside while you use receptive behavior to probe for information. Under what conditions might you disengage? Consider the possibility that you might succeed sooner than you expected to. Is there a way you can build on that to accomplish other influence objectives while you are on a roll, or should you end the meeting early and hope the other person doesn't feel that he or she has been a pushover?

Setting Yourself Up for Success

You can do a few things before you begin actively influencing the other person that will help you be successful. They may include

- Resolve old issues that may get in the way of working on new ones.
- Garner the support of people who are respected by the other.

- Choose a time when the other person will be most likely to be receptive (after a milestone has been achieved, during a time of day when he or she will not be distracted, etc.).
- Choose a place where the two of you can talk (actually or virtually) without interruptions or fear of arousing apprehension on the part of others.
- Let the other person know your motivation and intentions for the meeting.
- Do anything else you can think of that will put the other person at ease about the meeting, such as sending a detailed agenda or including someone he or she trusts in the invitation.
- Begin the meeting by expressing optimism about the results.
- Take time to do a "check-in" before you get down to business. Ask what's going on for the other person, whether he or she has anything to put on the agenda, or other questions that express an interest in him or her.
- Use behaviors that the other is most comfortable with to establish rapport at the beginning, even though your plan calls for you to use other behaviors to achieve your influence objective.

By taking some of these actions, you're not just trusting to luck or the other's good mood, but actively creating the conditions that give your plan the best possible chance for a successful outcome.

CHAPTER 15

Putting Your Plan to Work

Treating the Unexpected as an Opportunity

The one thing in the world of value is the active soul.
—Ralph Waldo Emerson

Improvisation

If practicing influence skills is like participating in a fitness program and planning for influence is like preparing for a journey, carrying out an influence plan is a lot like doing improvisational theater. You go in with a objective, some ideas about how to reach it, and a lot of knowledge about the situation. There is no script, however, and you're not the only actor. You have to respond to the lines the other players feed you and to the developing situation without losing track of where you want the performance to go. You have to be fast on your feet and flexible in your approach.

There are many lists of "improv rules," but here are a few that apply well to the practice of influence:

- *Always say, "Yes, and . . . "* Don't waste time disagreeing with or negating the other players. Instead, find something, even a small something, where you agree and build on that.

- *Show, don't tell.* Whenever possible, find an active, engaging way to demonstrate or prototype your idea or concept.

- *Treat mistakes or unexpected information as opportunities.* Take the new information and turn it in the direction of your objective. Acknowledge your own mistakes or misunderstandings openly and good-heartedly and find the humor in them.

- *Stay positive and flexible.* Allow yourself to be influenced and keep the performance moving toward a positive outcome for all.

Responding to New Information

No matter how carefully you plan, something will happen that you didn't expect. Influence is a dynamic process, and it isn't a monologue—there are other players. The approach that sounded great to your spouse may leave your manager cold. The rationale that you developed for your customer may be irrelevant, now that he has spoken to your competitor. Your teenage daughter may have obtained her counselor's support for her "sabbatical" idea. What do you do now?

Probably the best piece of advice I have ever received on the subject is also the simplest (although not the easiest) to apply. If what you're doing isn't working, stop doing it. Do nothing; do something—almost anything—different. But don't continue down the road you started on, because it will take you somewhere that you don't want to go. This is not as easy as it sounds. In fact, the more time you've spent preparing (and preparing is a good thing), the harder it might be for you to drop your plan and deal with the situation as it actually is. That's the paradox of planning, and why it's good to consider "what-ifs" when you plan.

Once you've stopped yourself, there are two ways to go. Here is where it's really helpful to know yourself as an influencer. If you're the kind of person who does best with some time to think before you act, go straight to the most important indirect influence technique (see Chapter 20) and *Disengage*. Be open about it, you'll get some credit for paying attention. And you'll keep your foot out of your mouth. Say, "That's interesting. I'd like to think about what you just told me. Let's get together again tomorrow" (or next week, this afternoon, even after a short break if time is pressing). Then think about your plan in the context of the new information and adjust it.

If you're the sort of influencer who thinks out loud, who does best by staying in the situation and working with it, go immediately to receptive behavior if you're not already there. Use *Inquire* and *Listen* behaviors and keep doing so until you have as much new information as you need. Then you can decide whether or not you want to disengage in order to confer with others or to redesign your approach.

Dealing with Defensiveness, Resistance, and Avoidance

You were only being reasonable, so why on earth did he get so defensive? Or why can't you schedule a meeting with your colleague to discuss this issue? Why is she always "too busy"? Why does your spouse have a last-minute reason not to go to every single meeting you've scheduled with the new contractor?

You will often be puzzled by the nature of someone's response to your attempts to influence him or her. He or she may not behave in the way that you planned or assumed that he or she would. And it's hard to treat this behavior as a valuable source of information (rather than a secret plot to make you crazy), but it is.

First, assume that the person is not actually bad, wrong, or stupid, but in fact is behaving in a way that makes perfect sense, given the way she or he understands the situation. In order to find that out so you can correct or deal with it, you can try to "reverse engineer" from the response to the interpretation. You can do that in two ways. Sometimes you can simply ask, in a neutral and curious way: "I've noticed that you haven't been able to make any of the meetings with the contractor. I wonder if there's a reason why you'd just as soon not see him right now?" If you do this, it's absolutely essential that the other person read the subtext (the unstated but important meaning) as saying, "You're a reasonable person, and I know you're behaving in a rational way. Help me understand it." Any hint of sarcasm or talking down to the other will be fatal to achieving your objective.

If direct influence is not available to you (the other person has left the room in a huff, slammed down the telephone, called you bad names, or simply hasn't been heard from for weeks), then you have another option. Think your way into his or her skin for a moment and ask yourself, "I'm reacting as if I have something to lose or something to fear; what is it?" Because defensive, resistant, and avoidance behavior is a normal, fight-or-flight mammalian self-protective response, the answer to that question is often quite clear. You may be surprised or hurt that the other person would think you were capable of something like that, but you will have to get over it if you want to influence. Don't make the person's misjudgment of you the issue. Instead, consider it an interesting, if incorrect, assumption and work with it, using curiosity rather than self-protection.

Once you have an idea of what's going on for the other person, you have a new influence opportunity: You'll need to convince her or him that you're not intending to do the thing that he or she fears. (Or if you are, you need to forget about influencing that person yourself. You can't influence others to appreciate and welcome what they see as threatening when you are the source of that threat.)

Managing Yourself

As much as I may see influence as an opportunity to affect the course of someone else's behavior, the only behavior I can affect directly is my own. The success or failure of an influence opportunity is determined, largely, by how well I can do that.

As part of your preparation, you will have examined your own wants, needs, attitudes, and assumptions related to this opportunity. In the actual situation, you'll put that information to work. For example, you'll notice when your own issues are getting in the way of moving toward your objective.

The following signs indicate that you need to manage your own behavior:

- You or the other person are experiencing a "fight-or-flight" reaction. Some signs of an excess of adrenaline in the system are external, such as an outburst of angry words or a threat to leave the room or the meeting; some are internal, physical stress responses such as a tight throat or gastrointestinal upset.
- The other person hasn't said anything for some time.
- You're moving further away from your objective as the conversation proceeds.
- The other person is becoming more resistant or defensive.
- You're acting as if your objective was to make the other person wrong.

Sometimes the best way to manage yourself and the situation is to disengage temporarily (see Chapter 20) and reflect on what's going on—you may be able to return with a more productive approach. In any case, you'll be more in charge of yourself. You can sometimes ask the other person to take a time-out with you, discuss the way the meeting or conversation is going, and think of a better way to proceed. This must be done in an objective way. Blaming the other person for the problems you're having in influencing him or her will only escalate those problems. Even in very difficult situations, asking for feedback and/or disclosing can turn the situation around. For example, I've found that if I notice that I'm becoming excessively self-righteous or defensive and call myself on it before the other person does, this action invariably brings a measure of good humor to the conversation. This can clear the way for influence to occur.

One of the most effective and most difficult self-management tasks is that of consciously making the other person look more intelligent, more reasonable, more well-intentioned than you believe him or her to be. It's one exaggeration that will work to your benefit as an influencer. People tend to live up—or down—to your expectations of them.

In summary, managing yourself is perhaps the most difficult aspect of being an effective influencer. It requires an ability to acknowledge your own ego needs and tendencies toward self-deception and to treat them with gentleness and a certain affectionate humor, without being limited by them. In other words, you have to be a grownup about influence in order to keep your inner child from throwing a tantrum at the wrong time or hiding in the closet for fear of punishment.

The Uses of Silence

One of the most underused and effective influence techniques is that of keeping your mouth shut. We humans have a habit of getting in our own way by stepping on the other person's lines or interrupting his or her thought process. We're sometimes so afraid of silence that we answer our own questions and argue both sides of an issue, thereby doing the other person's work (and not, it goes without saying, influencing anyone but ourselves).

The most important ideas we express, the most important questions that we ask, need to be followed by enough silence to allow the other person time to consider (especially if he or she is a classic introvert and likes to think before responding). In fact, this silence can be where influence occurs, because in the end, influence happens in the other person.

Mostly, we don't let the silence happen because we're afraid of being interrupted. We're concerned that we might forget where we were going, that the other will take the lead in the conversation. Remember under those circumstances that, if you've done your planning, you'll be confident enough to find your way back to leading or guiding the conversation, once again, toward your objective. And, because influence is always a dialogue, you may learn something in the process.

Making It Up on the Fly

In our fast-paced lives, opportunities for influence come and go in a flash. You won't always have time to plan. Still, there are a few things that you can keep in mind to help you when you have to take influence action on the fly.

- Think of what your objective is for the interaction and then keep it in front of you. If it seems to be retreating into the distance, change course.
- Maintain a balance between expressive and receptive behavior. If you're not making progress, switch to the other kind.

- Never say or do anything that makes the other look or feel bad, wrong, or stupid, especially if there are other people around.
- Treat resistance as a source of information.
- Be curious rather than defensive.

And remember, if what you are doing isn't working, stop doing it. Nothing works all the time, even with the same person or in the same situation. In day-to-day influence, the best approach is akin to the scientific method. Know what you want to achieve, make an educated guess about how best to achieve it, experiment actively, be objective about the outcome, and be ready to try again until you succeed or realize that you're not going to accomplish the result you hope for.

In Part III, we'll examine some special issues in influence: The ethical implications of being an active influencer, the use of electronic and social media to influence, influencing your team, the means for influencing indirectly, what research in neuroscience and behavioral economics can teach us, and some ideas for next steps in your growth as an active influencer.

Special Issues in Influence

PART

III

Special Issues in Influence

The Ethics of Influence

Doing Well by Doing Good

The moral sense is always supported by the permanent interest of the parties.
Else, I know not how, in our world, any good would ever get done.
—Ralph Waldo Emerson

Manipulation versus Influence

In our *Exercising Influence*™ workshops, the issue of manipulation often arises. Many people are concerned about the ethical implications of being conscious and tactical about influence. There is some confusion about the distinction between manipulation and influence. A thesaurus suggests the following distinction: to *manipulate* is to maneuver, handle, exploit, or deceive. To *influence* is to induce, incite, persuade, or activate. Influence implies respect for the other; manipulation does not. There is nothing fundamentally unethical or dishonest about choosing your behavior and words deliberately in order to persuade or activate others to join you in taking action.

When asked the question, "How do you know that you have been manipulated?" groups of managers and leaders consistently say, "When the other has been dishonest with me, leading me to take an action I would not have taken otherwise." When asked, "How do you know that you have been influenced?"

the typical reply is, "I voluntarily choose to change or take action based on what the other did or said."

Thus, there are two key issues that distinguish one from the other: (1) trust in the honesty of the influencer and (2) a sense of choice about the action. Influence implies individual choice based on trustworthy information and guidance. Manipulation happens in the shadows or under the table, influence happens in the open.

Several factors may cause people to be manipulative. Sometimes it's simply a skill or experience deficit; we're doing what has been done to us. Sometimes we wish to avoid the appearance of using direct power and hope that people will believe they're making a real choice even though they are not. Sometimes we're fearful of the conflict that may result from telling the truth, so we maintain a hidden agenda and hope things go our way without having to reveal it. Sometimes we simply haven't done our homework and are choosing an expedient way to involve another person. And there are certain pathological personality disorders that lead some people to be consistently manipulative.

Expressive influence becomes manipulative when we

- Make up or distort facts to support our positions.
- Imply that we share goals that we do not, in fact, share.
- Take credit for others' ideas.
- Promise things that we know we can't deliver.
- Make threats we don't have the power or will to carry out.
- Imply that powerful others will take actions (the equivalent of "wait until your father comes home") without having checked this out in advance.
- Fail to warn the other of important consequences of taking or not taking an action.
- Express a vision that we know to be unrealistic or impossible to achieve or that we don't really believe in.
- Flatter the other insincerely to encourage him or her to join or support us.

Receptive influence becomes manipulative when we

- Ask for information, then use it to harm or embarrass the other.
- Twist the other's words, intentions, or motivations in the guise of listening and attempting to understand.
- Show false empathy when we in fact are judgmental.
- Invite the other to be open and vulnerable without reciprocating.

- Imply in a subtle or sarcastic way that the other is bad, wrong, or stupid to believe as he or she does (rather than initiating an open discussion of differences).
- Reject any ideas or suggestions the other comes up with in response, unless and until we hear the "right answer."
- Invite the other to take action as if it were his or her responsibility, and then use power, sarcasm, or ridicule to attempt to stop him or her from taking the action.

The ethical influencer must ask him or herself the following questions

- Am I telling the literal truth, as far as I know, where any objective data is involved? Have I left out any key information that the other should know before making a choice?
- Am I being honest about my own opinions, beliefs, intentions, enthusiasm, and commitment when I have expressed them? Have I been open about my intention to influence the other?
- Am I willing and do I have the option to take "no" for an answer?
- Am I willing and do I have the option to allow the other to take a different action from the one I would prefer?
- Is this an issue that can best be dealt with through influence rather than the use of direct power that I have or can borrow? If not, am I willing to use that power openly?

Influence and Self-Interest

One of the great ethical responsibilities of the influencer is to be aware of his or her motivation in relation to the influence goal. It's perfectly legitimate to serve your own interests as long as you're not working against the interests of those you choose to influence or of the institutions or systems of which you are both members and to whom you owe respect and loyalty. Thus, influencing someone to disobey a legitimate rule or law (one you were both aware of and, in essence, signed up to uphold) can be unethical, whereas influencing someone to work with you to change a rule or law you believe to be unfair would be ethical. Influencing someone to help you do something that would benefit you but could be harmful to him or her would be unethical, unless you were completely honest about the risks involved and the person had free choice.

It's also important not to misuse your knowledge of others' self-interest or vulnerability to guide them in a direction you know would have serious negative consequences for them or others.

What Doesn't Work

I think the behaviors that I'm going to name below are not only ineffective, but also unethical, although often done with the best of intentions. These actions are based on the unexamined assumption that other people are mean, foolish, fearful, or unimportant and don't deserve to be treated with respect. They include

- Threatening
- Whining
- Tit-for-tat
- Ridiculing
- Shaming
- Anything else that attempts to make the other look or feel bad, wrong, or stupid

When these behaviors work, it's only while you're watching, and only if you have sufficient power. None of them actually influences anyone, since influence is something that requires the participation and agreement of the other.

In the long run, anything we gain from these unethical or ineffective practices is likely to be short-lived, lead to a loss of trust or reputation, harm the influence relationship, and be detrimental to our self-perception.

CHAPTER 17

Influencing Electronically

The Wonders and Terrors of Instant Communication

Words are also actions, and actions are a kind of words.
—Ralph Waldo Emerson

Welcome to the (Too Much) Information Age

There is nothing that will make the effects of a vacation or long weekend disappear faster than the realization that we have hundreds of messages to deal with. The electronic networks that were supposed to make our lives easier and more efficient have become sticky spiderwebs of complexities that attract and trap time and effort.

Because of the mobility of many families, electronic media have become more and more important in communicating with one another. With children who are away at college, spouses and partners who are doing business in another part of the world, parents who have retired and moved, and siblings and friends who live far away, our personal lives are also filled with opportunities to influence electronically.

At work, many of us belong to teams with members scattered across the globe, many of whom we may never meet in person. We frequently participate in video-, web-, or teleconferences. Leaders and those who report to them may be based in very different time zones, with little opportunity for face-to-face conversations. Our workday can stretch to accommodate our global team, partners, or customers.

Like it or not, we live in a world in which we must communicate with and influence people whom we seldom see. Realistically, much of our communication, and thus much of our influencing, will take place through these channels. We might as well learn to do it in the most effective way we can.

Electronic influence can be synchronous (in real time) or asynchronous (participants can communicate intermittently at their own convenience). Each has advantages and disadvantages related to the immediacy of the need. Synchronous media, such as teleconferences, text, chat, or IMs, can be positive when it's important to find support or make team decisions quickly. However, teleconferences or web meetings can lose effectiveness when members multitask or zone out during important discussions. Video meetings can work better, at least with small groups. The more senses that you can involve, the more engaged participants are likely to be.

Influencing asynchronously, such as through e-mail, is challenging and should probably not be your first choice for important opportunities if other means are at hand. In some organizations, people who sit in adjacent offices or cubicles will send e-mails in preference to speaking directly, especially about difficult issues. Unfortunately, the perceived importance, and thus the impact of a message, is often directly related to the effort and risk the sender has put forth.

Some situations in which e-mail is not a good means of communicating or influencing include

- When the issue is complex or urgent and the other person is potentially accessible
- When there is a conflict involved and the other person may see you as attempting to avoid it
- When you want the other person to understand how important the issue is to you
- When you want the other person to recognize how important his or her opinion is to you
- When you need time to draw the other person out in order to gain his or her ideas and support

In all of these cases and others, it's best if you can arrange a face-to-face meeting or, if that is not possible, a video chat or telephone meeting.

A common problem with e-mail, in particular, is that people tend to treat it as if it were a conversation and don't plan or screen their remarks. Once a message has been sent, it's difficult to unsend it. And you don't know how many other people have had an opportunity to eavesdrop on the conversation. Voice mail and e-mail differ from real-time, instant communication in that there's a record left that can be shared with others—at times, including those for whom the message was not intended. You would think that everyone from business and political leaders to terrorists would have figured this out by now, yet scandals or scoops based on intercepted electronic communications continue at this writing.

E-mail (and voice mail—less used now than in the past, but still possible in most organizations) in general follows the same principles of influence as in face-to-face influence opportunities. The behaviors are the same, although you don't have the reinforcement of voice tone (with e-mail), facial expressions, or gestures to clarify the meaning of your words. Over time, you should balance expressive and receptive influence; you can often include both types of behavior in the same message. In fact, it's often a good idea to err on the side of receptive behavior, since you have fewer clues as to how the other person is reacting than you do in face-to-face interactions. Video chats provide a broader band of information and thus are particularly valuable with people who are new to one another. Once you have become more "real" to one another, two-way influence is usually easier.

Learning how to use these media in conscious and productive ways can greatly expand your sphere of influence. While many people today communicate continually through electronic means, few have developed the skills to use these influence opportunities well. Failing to do so can lead not only to missed opportunities, but also to unprecedented and costly misunderstandings and conflicts.

First, You Have to Get Their Attention

Influence messages require a response so that you know whether you're getting closer to or further from your objective. Among the large number of asynchronous communications most business people receive daily, only a few will earn a thoughtful response. Given limitations of time and energy, we tend to select the ones that look most important or interesting.

These will probably include

- Messages from people who are key to our success or with whom we have an important relationship
- Messages about something in which we have an immediate interest or strong need

- Messages that look as if we will not get into trouble by the way we respond
- Messages that can be responded to easily and quickly
- Messages that are sent to us personally, rather than to a long list
- Messages that are brief and succinct; large blocks of text are not likely to invite the recipient to review the message quickly

We're unlikely to respond quickly or productively to messages when we perceive that our responses will create problems or more work for us, provide no benefits, or have no impact on anything we care about.

Knowing this, it's possible to design messages so they are more likely to attract the recipient's attention. First, the recipient must be interested enough to open the message rather than ignore it. Next, he or she must read and respond to it. The subject line of your message should influence the recipient to open and read it, if your name alone won't do it (and it probably won't unless you are the person's boss, best friend, or current romantic interest). A subject line that reads, "I need your inspirations about a topic for the meeting," for example, will probably get a better hearing than, "Why haven't I heard from you?" Electronic whining is still whining.

Let the other person know up-front, in the first line or two, what you need and why he or she would benefit from responding to your message. For example, "Tell me where you think we should hold our next meeting. I want to make sure you don't have to travel as far as you did last month. I need to book the meeting by Friday." In this case, the response needed is clear, the benefits are obvious, and the deadline is specific. If it's necessary to send a long message electronically, breaking the message into shorter segments through the use of bullets or numbered lists can help.

Anything you can do to make it easy to respond by chat, phone, or return e-mail, such as offering options A, B, or C, will make it easier and thus more likely that you'll receive a response. When you leave a message on voice mail, it may be helpful to brief (and it should be very brief!) the person on the issue, then say that there's no need to call back unless a discussion is needed, and that, otherwise, you will assume the other person accepts or supports the idea or will attend the meeting or commit to the responsibility. This works best with relatively simple and noncontroversial messages; it can save time and is useful in uncovering areas of disagreement of which you were not aware.

Stimulating a Productive Response

As in any other form of influencing, you'll want to avoid creating defensiveness. Using words that are accusatory or inflammatory will create a fight-or-flight reaction, just as it would in real time. Either you will not hear back from the person, or you'll hear something you would rather not have heard. In either case, no influence will occur.

Use words that are nonjudgmental, businesslike, and that assume that the other will respond productively. Snide or snarky messages are easy to ignore. It also helps to acknowledge your understanding that it will require some time and effort on the other's part, but avoid obsequiousness.

A *good example*: "I know you're on a tight deadline. Let me know a good time to get ten minutes with you to review the report."

A *bad example*: "I suppose you'll be too busy to meet with me again."

Preventing Misunderstandings, Embarrassment, and Other E-mail Disasters

All of us have heard stories of e-mail disasters, such as the man who sent his girlfriend a very explicit love letter and accidentally copied it to everyone in the company. Most e-mail disasters, however, occur because we "write out loud" and then press the "send" button without thinking about how the other might react, or whether this message will help achieve an influence objective.

The one certain way to prevent such occurrences is to leave some time between composing an important e-mail message—one that is intended to influence—and sending it. This is almost an unnatural act, given the instantaneous nature of most e-mail communication, but it has many benefits.

A good exercise is to write the message as a first draft, then set it aside for a while. (Even a few minutes can help.) Reread it and ask yourself the following questions:

- What is my influence objective here?
- Am I using the most effective possible behaviors to achieve that objective? What might work better?
- Is there a balance between expressive and receptive influence?
- What other interpretations of my words might be possible? Is there any possibility the other person might be put off or made defensive by any of these interpretations? What is the "worst case" interpretation he or she might make?

Err on the pessimistic side of things; it is amazing what people can read into messages if they're having a particularly paranoid sort of day. Once you have identified all possible misunderstandings (or, for that matter, correct understandings that won't help you reach your objective—yes, you really do think the marketing VP is a yo-yo, but you have to do business with him!), you will want to rewrite the message. Send a really important influence message only when you've reviewed it at least twice (and sometimes it's good to have someone else whom you trust look at it as well).

Virtual Teams: Culture and Context

These days, many of us participate in global, virtual teams. We're also more and more likely to belong to families with diverse cultural backgrounds. Since much of our communication with global colleagues, family, and friends is done through electronic means, it's useful to educate ourselves in cross-cultural norms regarding communication and influence as applied to virtual meetings as well as e-mail and messaging. Edward T. Hall, a well-known anthropologist in the twentieth century, suggested terms that describe two different types of culture:*

- High-context cultures, such as Thailand, in which members share a good deal of unspoken but understood meaning. People in these cultures tend to use fewer words to communicate or influence, assuming that the other will know what he or she wants to express or ask for. Relationships tend to be highly valued and feelings may be expressed in a nuanced way. There is more focus on the group and mutual support is expected.
- Low-context cultures, such as Germany, in which members make no such assumptions and tend to explain their meaning in detail. There is greater focus on facts and logic, more individualism, less reliance on traditional ways of doing things, and needs are expressed more directly.

It's no surprise that these differences can create difficulty in face-to-face conversations as well as virtual ones. In fact, even when the organizational culture is held constant, such as in the work of Geert Hofstede,† the differences between national and ethnic cultures remain. If you are part of such a team, it may be worthwhile to do some cultural research or find a "coach" who's familiar with one or more of the other cultures represented on your team, so you can minimize cultural misunderstandings.

---

*Edward T. Hall, *Beyond Culture* (New York: Anchor Books, 1976).
†Geert Hofstede, *Culture's Consequences: Comparing Values, Behaviors, Institutions, and Organizations Across Nations*, 2nd ed. (Thousand Oaks, CA: SAGE Publications, 2001).

Texts, Instant Messaging, and Beyond

Instant messages and texts are ubiquitous and insistent. They can be especially useful when you want to point the recipient toward a longer important message that you send in another way. Instant messaging creates the opportunity for a conversation in real time and can certainly be used to influence others. Taking time to review your response before sending, as you would with e-mail, only faster, is the key to effective influence using IMs or texts.

Our continuous connection to our mobile devices means that we live in a world where influence can happen with anyone, anywhere, at any time. (For the introverts among us, this may not be good news.)

Influencing through Social Media

Expanding Your Sphere of Influence

Great hearts steadily send forth the secret forces that incessantly draw great events.

—Ralph Waldo Emerson

From One to Many

While this book is primarily focused on influencing one person or a small group, social media now make it possible to influence many people directly with the same message. In fact, the people who are most effective at getting their messages across in this way are called "influencers."

Social media sites provide a way to form new influence relationships, to learn from others, and to make your voice heard within communities you belong to and care about. Many users see these sites primarily as a communication tool to stay in touch with friends and family, as a way of learning about or offering career or job opportunities, or as a way to expand their mailing lists. Others, though, see in these sites the potential for building their reputation, for providing access to people and groups that they might never otherwise meet, and for two-way influence on topics that are important to their success.

It's especially important to be clear as to why you're choosing this means to influence others. Since it's one to many and you have limited control as to who may eventually read or hear about it, make sure you've thought carefully about your influence goal, your key influence targets, and why you see social media and this site in particular as an important way to reach them.

How to Become a Social Media "Influencer"

Membership has its privileges, but in order to gain the greatest value from this new influence opportunity, it's important to take direct action. Here are a few ways you can use social media to increase your influence impact:

- Sign up for or become active on social media sites related to your personal or professional focus.
- Connect to key colleagues and follow important "influencers."
- Join and post in groups that share your interests.
- Respond to other's posts and engage in conversations with them.
- Invite people with similar interests to connect.
- Start conversations in groups and contribute frequently to the ones you're following.
- Choose a topic that's timely and relevant and write a short, well-researched or thought-through article. Post a link to it in groups that may be interested.
- If you don't have a personal website, consider setting one up where you can post all of your articles so that when a topic arises that you've written about, you can refer people to your website.
- Share articles that others have written that interest you and might help move people in a direction you believe in.
- Engage in public conversations with people who see things differently so that you can influence people who are currently undecided toward your point of view.
- Follow the rules of the group such as not marketing or selling your books or services.
- Be clear about what your objective is in participating on social media.

Writing an Influential Post or Article

Some of the suggestions in the previous chapter on influencing through electronic means are also relevant to social media. For example, just as you should write a compelling subject line to make sure someone opens your e-mail message, choose a title for your post that will catch the attention of the people you want to influence. While you're sending a message that is potentially one to many, that only happens if people are influenced to read it!

When posting on professional sites, such as LinkedIn, you'll need to strike the right balance. You'll want to show that you are knowledgeable and have something of value to share without coming across as simply trying to drive sales of your book or visits to your website. The most well-received and influential posts seem to have two things in common: (1) a well–thought-through reply to the question posed or to an earlier response (often giving credit to the author of that post by name) and (2) a certain generosity of spirit. This is evidenced by several things—including, but not limited to

- Providing personal and specific stories of how you've dealt with the issue.
- Sharing mistakes and failures and the learning that resulted from them.
- Offering to share resources that were helpful to you either by linking to them or inviting people to contact you in order to receive them (and not following that with a constant stream of marketing messages).
- Supporting and reinforcing the thoughts of others in the stream (by name) and encouraging others to read their posts or links.
- When writing an article, your main goal is to make it interesting enough for people to want to share with their friends and colleagues, thus introducing new people to your thought leadership. Tackle this as you would any opportunity to publish your work—that means:
  - Create a succinct title that reflects the content.
  - Make sure to give proper credit to other authors or researchers whose work you refer to or quote.
  - Edit your work carefully—or ask someone else to do so—so you're sure it's free of typos, poor grammar, misplaced apostrophes, misspellings, and all the other oh-so-human errors that can cause people to devalue your work.
  - Keep it brief and use the first paragraph to give readers a sense of what they'll gain from reading the whole article.

- When possible, use stories and examples to illustrate your points—the human brain is wired to learn from stories.

- Point people to your article through other social media sites and ask others who like your work to do the same.

The phenomenon of social media seems as if it creates a new venue for influence. In fact, it simply provides an expanded marketplace for ideas. The best ideas, sadly, don't always have the greatest influence impact. The marketplace is crowded, and there's a lot of competition. But by focusing on communicating your best ideas in a clear, professional, and interesting way, and being thoughtful about where, when, and how you display them, you can use social media to expand your network and your social influence.

Applied Influence

Making Things Happen

This time, like all times, is a very good one, if we but know what to do with it.
— Ralph Waldo Emerson

Maintaining and Improving Your Influence Fitness

You have developed your influence skills, mapped the territory, prepared, and implemented your plan for a specific influence situation. By now, you probably know whether this is a set of skills you really want to develop. As in any fitness program, your progress will depend on your willingness to be conscious, focused, and disciplined about regular practice. Ideally, as in a gym or fitness center, you will start with some simple, low-impact exercises and move on to ones that are more complex and risky as you become more skillful. If you want to become more powerful, graceful, and flexible as an influencer, there is no better exercise than to decide on an objective and consciously go after it. Following are some ideas to think about and some experiments to try at work, at home, and in your community.

Making Things Happen at Work

A component of making things happen at work is the recognition that comes with being seen as an effective influencer. In today's flatter, more team-based organizations, leadership through influence is highly respected and valued. It's reasonable to expect that effective influence behavior will be related to career success. But, because it requires a willingness to take risks, to be open about, and to stand up for your ideas and opinions, it also exposes you to jealousy and competitiveness. You will fail more often because you are initiating action more often. You'll find it difficult to become less visible, even if you want to be.

A frequently cited *Fortune* magazine article by Ram Charan and Geoffrey Colvin* suggested that one thing unsuccessful CEOs had in common was a "failure to execute." (I did think that was rather obvious until I thought of a few failed CEOs who had executed the wrong thing only too well.) I would revise that to suggest that executives and other leaders fail most when they have a good idea and are unable to influence others to own it and make it happen.

Try This at Work

Here are some suggestions about using your influence skills at work. Try one or two of them every day in a conscious way, and take a minute afterward to reflect on how the interaction went and what you learned from doing it. If you choose to influence someone with whom you are in a high-trust relationship, ask for feedback. Acknowledge that you're working on being more effective as an influencer. Ask what he or she noticed about your approach and how you could be more effective.

- Influence a co-worker to reschedule a meeting that is inconvenient for you.
- Influence a team member to take on another responsibility.
- Influence your manager to send you to an important professional conference.
- Influence your client to extend a deadline for deliverables.
- Influence your manager to implement a change in the way projects are assigned.
- Influence a decision maker to use a vendor that you prefer.
- Influence a colleague to substitute for you at a meeting.
- Influence your manager to provide more resources for your project.
- Influence a direct report to take on additional responsibilities.
- Influence a peer to support your controversial proposal.
- Influence a colleague to help you meet a deadline on an important project.
- Influence a senior manager in another part of the organization to sponsor an innovative idea.

---

*Ram Charan and Geoffrey Colvin, "Why CEOs Fail," *Fortune*, June 21, 1999, p. 68.

The next time a colleague or manager turns down your request, try using receptive behavior (*Inquire* or *Facilitate*) to learn what is in the way or what it would take for him or her to say "yes" to you; then use *Negotiate* behavior to firm up an agreement.

Making Things Happen at Home

By contrast, you will usually want to make things happen at home through influence without being recognized as the "mover and shaker." You will probably go out of your way to balance the influence relationships in your family or household (this is not the same as balancing the power relationships, which is not appropriate in families with young children). You have an opportunity to model a way of accomplishing results that helps everyone in the household feel both involved and committed and to develop a set of skills that will pay lifelong dividends. If there are children in the household, you will be offering them the invaluable gift of learning how to make things happen in their own lives in a way that is respectful of others, empowering to themselves and the family, and productive of results.

It's a good idea to let people who are close to you know up-front that you are going to be trying some new approaches and to enlist them in supporting you. Even though a partner, spouse, or friend might have been telling you that you should change, when you then do, it requires something different in the way of a response from them. Humans are paradoxical creatures, and sometimes we prefer behavior that is "the devil we know" to something that is unfamiliar, even though we have asked for the change. This can sometimes lead to a lack of support for positive change on your part that you will find surprising and painful. If you keep important others "in the loop" from the beginning, they will have time to get used to the idea, feel included in the process, and be more likely to offer the encouragement and feedback that you need.

Try This at Home

There are many opportunities daily to influence the people you live with or to whom you are close. Here are a few ideas to start with:

- Influence a family member to take on a new household responsibility.
- Influence your spouse or partner to try a new restaurant or see a movie that would normally not appeal to him or her.
- Influence a child to reduce "screen time" by an hour per day.
- Influence a spouse, partner, or friend to take responsibility for weekend plans.

- Influence an older child to keep you better informed about his or her whereabouts.

- Influence a spouse, partner, or friend to take a vacation to a destination that is new to both of you.

- Influence a friend or family member to cook a meal for you.

- Influence a partner, friend, or spouse to invest with you in a business opportunity.

- Influence a young family member or friend to apply to a specific college or academic program that you believe would be a good fit.

- Influence a spouse or partner to purchase a home or vacation property.

- Influence a young person to tell you about a dream he or she has for the future or a problem he or she is experiencing.

- Influence an elderly parent to stop driving.

- Influence a household member to fix the broken "whatsit" that you have all been putting up with for several months.

The next time you and a spouse, partner, or other family member start into a familiar conflict that usually ends in an impasse, interrupt the process by using receptive behavior (*Inquire, Listen,* or *Attune*) to understand his or her needs, concerns, issues, or point of view.

Making Things Happen in Your Community

Making things happen in your community means that you will be asked to do so again and again. Fortunately, if you are an effective influencer, you will not have to do it alone. You will have the support of people who are willing to put effort into things that you and they care about. Very few things that we care about in our communities can be accomplished alone. By using your influence skills, you will help create a network of people who will continue the important work.

Try This in Your Community

Here are some possible influence opportunities in your community. You will think of many more.

- Influence an important person to speak to your organization or serve on your committee.

- Influence a department of your local government or association to give you permission to build a nonconforming addition to your house.

- Influence a friend or neighbor to join you in promoting or sponsoring a community event.
- Influence your child's teacher to allow him or her to accompany you on a vacation trip outside of school holidays.
- Influence a group of neighbors to join together in obtaining permission for and creating a community garden on an empty lot in your neighborhood.
- Influence a clergy member in your church, mosque, temple, or synagogue to preach a sermon on a topic of interest to you.
- Influence your local government or association to change or modify a regulation that is inconvenient or unnecessary.
- Influence your neighbor to attend a meeting on a topic of interest to you.
- Influence others in your community to donate to a cause that you believe to be important.

The next time you're disappointed in the kind of service or response you are receiving from an organization or official in your community, use expressive influence to voice your concerns and all the influence skills at your disposal to gain others' support in changing the situation.

Influence skills, like all skills, are developed through practice, feedback, and re-practice. By finding opportunities to influence and consciously choosing and using these skills every day, your "influence muscles" will continue to grow stronger. Just as you need to cool down after exercising in the gym, you can cool down after exercising influence by reflecting on the experience. Think about what worked and what did not and decide how to take that learning forward to the next opportunity.

Influencing Indirectly

Influencing beyond Your Boundaries

The best effect of fine persons is felt after we have left their presence.
—Ralph Waldo Emerson

What Is Indirect Influence?

Indirect influence means simply that you keep your influence objective in mind and take some action other than dealing directly with the person or group whom you wish to influence. This can mean either that you work through other people or that you use other means to accomplish your objective. Indirect influence is normally done in the open, however, and should not be confused with manipulation, in which your motivations and agenda are intentionally hidden.

When Is Indirect Influence Appropriate?

Most of the time it will be easier to influence others directly. Here are some situations in which that may not be as effective:

- You don't have access to the target person or group because of political, geographic, language, cultural, or other considerations.
- You don't currently have a good influence relationship with the other person, and the issue is urgent enough that you don't have the time to build one.

117

- You are not perceived by the other to have the relevant knowledge, expertise, or status that would be the appropriate power sources for this influence issue.
- The issue is a major one, and you simply don't have the power to be effective directly.
- You have been using direct methods and have hit a snag or are at an impasse.

These situations and others like them will lead you to consider other means of influencing.

Influencing through Other Individuals

Sometimes the best solution is to find someone who is in a better position to influence the target person than you are and delegate the influencing to him or her. (Of course, this will require you to influence that person to take on the responsibility of influencing the target person or group.)

If this is your best option, be sure to discuss your influence objective very thoroughly with the other person and give him or her the benefit of the planning work you have done. You're giving up some control of the specific outcome in exchange for the chance to achieve your objective, so it's essential that you trust the other person and share all relevant information, including your own areas of flexibility. You should also be very open to this person's advice regarding your objective; he or she will have to believe in it to be able to achieve it for you or your team.

Influencing as Part of a Group

When an issue is extremely important or affects a great many people, or when the influence target is at some political or hierarchical distance, you may want to consider organizing a group in order to influence. One middle manager's opinion may not count for much with the COO, but a cross-functional committee of concerned managers may be able to get a hearing. One son or daughter may not be able to convince an elderly parent to give up the privilege of driving, but all the siblings acting in concert may be effective.

It often takes not only a large number but also a broad coalition of people and vested interests to influence senior corporate or government officials to take action or change course. On the one hand, it's easy to dismiss a small homogeneous group as "a bunch of cranks," but much more difficult to do so when they represent diverse aspects of the community. On the other hand, recent research suggests that change can happen rapidly when the right people with a powerful idea "tip the balance."

Debate as an Indirect Influence Tactic

Debate is a common approach to persuasion, but one that doesn't work well as a direct influence tactic. This often comes as a surprise to people, especially those who are more analytical. Although debating an issue can develop strong ideas and make sure that bad ideas don't go unchallenged, it's usually a contest of ideas and positions with winners and losers. However, it can be useful as an indirect influence approach. The greatest influence impact is on those who are listening to and/or judging the debate. Since most debate is focused on proving that one's position is right and the other's position is wrong, the debaters are likely to become more firmly fixed in the rightness of their cause or opinion, rather than influencing one another. Research has shown that rational argument is of little use against strongly held convictions. Thus, there is little hope of influencing the other debater, but you can hold a debate with another person as a way of influencing a third party. This works best, of course, if both debaters are aware that this is the purpose of the debate.

Disengaging as a Means to an End

Disengaging can be an effective way to manage time, authority issues, and relationships. Sometimes moving away temporarily can help you to reach a satisfactory outcome when moving forward would only create greater resistance or loss of an opportunity.

Sometimes it's useful to maintain your individual connection to the influence target but move to a different set of tactics. For example, when you're at an impasse (or, preferably, when you see that you are headed in that direction but before it occurs), you can choose to disengage temporarily. My husband, who is particularly good at this tactic, used to say in a line reminiscent of a popular commercial for wine, "Let's make no decision before its time; we can discuss this later." Artfully, he always manages to do this just before I've committed to an absolute "no" on the issue. This tactic allows the use of persistence and timing to have its effect. When you choose to disengage, it's important to let the other know that you'll be back—and often to establish when you will reconvene. This prevents disengagement from looking like retreat.

Of course, there will be times when you recognize that there is no point in continuing an influence attempt, given the time and energy it looks as if it will take compared to the likelihood and value of success. In that case, disengagement may be permanent. (It may also provide an opportunity to refocus your influence plan on a more appropriate objective or a different person.) You can still gain some influence value from such a situation by being graceful rather than huffy about it.

"I can see that this issue is of great importance to you. As long as you're willing to take the major responsibility for seeing that it gets done, I'm willing to do it your way." Then let go of the issue completely, rather than wait in hiding until something goes wrong so you can say, "I told you so." You'll pay for that. This is an example of "disarming" or letting go of issues that are more important to the other than to you and saving your influence energy for issues that you care about more. On the one hand, this may create a sense of fairness and reasonableness that you can call on later. On the other hand, you may be better off using such opportunities for more direct negotiation. A quid pro quo that is a done deal is more effective than "you owe me one"—something that is almost never remembered in the same way by both parties.

Using Other Means to Influence Indirectly

When you don't have access to a "subject-matter expert" and the issue involves knowledge that the other person doesn't think you have, influencing through websites, books, and articles by people that he or she respects may be helpful. This is better done early in the process, however, rather than as an "I told you so" attempt, which is likely to inspire a defensive and resistant response.

Finally, one of the most useful indirect influence tools (a form of disengaging briefly) is the use of humor. Knowing when to use a story, joke, or wry comment to relieve tension or keep the encounter from going too far in the wrong direction is an art. But there is one clear rule about the use of humor in influencing. It should *never* be used in a sarcastic manner or in any way that might reflect negatively on the other person or something he or she holds dear. It should be either slightly self-deprecating or directed at a force or third party that you both consider a "common enemy." And you must also be artful about bringing the conversation back toward where you want it to go.

Influencing Your Team

From One to Many

Trust men and they will be true to you; treat them greatly and they will show themselves great.

—Ralph Waldo Emerson

Expanding Your Influence Impact

Teams (as well as families or other close groups) are, by their nature, influence organizations. In today's organizations, teams, both co-located and virtual, are usually made up of people with different professional skills, a different set of information and ideas, and with different formal reporting relationships. As a result, the direct use of power is seldom an option. Whether you're a team leader or a team member, you'll need to influence others on your team to agree on goals and milestones, provide information, resolve problems or conflicts, offer or share resources, take on added responsibilities, and implement ideas or proposals. Team projects can't be completed without agreements, yet innovation and excellence will only result from a free flow of ideas and active influencing in all directions. Influencing a team involves all the skills required for one-to-one influence but is a more complex and multi-layered process.

Establish a Climate for Influence

The process of team influence begins with the formation of the team. Among the first things a team needs to accomplish are to

- Create a team vision of success.
- Articulate the values upon which they will base decisions.
- Establish goals and milestones for projects.
- Agree on norms or ground rules for how the team will operate.
- Build processes and forums for sharing information and ideas.

These steps can create a climate of mutual trust and respect that encourages active influencing. For example, once a team has created a vision of success, that vision can be the basis for keeping the group aligned. A vision to which members have made a real commitment can be a powerful energy source for influence. Common goals and values provide a basis for demonstrating the benefits of a proposal. Norms and ground rules that encourage sharing of ideas, open discussion, listening to others' ideas, and questioning the status quo encourage influence exchanges in all directions.

Team leaders can demonstrate their openness to influence during meetings and actively encourage members' productive influence behaviors. During an early team meeting, the leader can tell members how best to influence him or her and encourage or ask other members to do the same.

Do Your Homework

When you have an important idea or proposal to put before the team, you will greatly increase your probability of success by careful preparation. Some or all of the following steps will be necessary in order to gain team support for an important, yet controversial proposal.

- Identify the members who will be the opinion leaders regarding your proposal. Who will people look to for guidance as to whether to accept, reject, or modify your ideas?

- Meet with each of the opinion leaders and learn what their issues and decision criteria will be. Use *Inquiring* and *Listening* behaviors to get as much information as you can before committing to an influence approach. This is especially important when you expect opposition from a person who is influential with others. Consulting with that person ahead of time will be educational at the least, and the involvement may even lead to your developing a proposal that can garner this person's support.

- Modify your proposal to take account of others' issues and concerns. Create a better fit between your idea and the team's vision. Think about how your proposal supports the values and goals the team has agreed upon.

- Do the necessary research to support your proposal; look for data that will be meaningful to the opinion leaders and others on the team.

- Frame your proposal so that each opinion leader can see how it meets his or her decision criteria. There are usually several ways to look at the issues. Be flexible in seeing your proposal through the eyes of each of the others. At the same time, make sure that you maintain the integrity of the core idea.

- Meet with opinion leaders and do your best to enlist their support before the meeting where you plan to present your proposal to the entire team. Listen to their response and be prepared to modify your proposal where you believe you can, in order to gain their support. Rather than diluting your proposal, this can actually have the effect of strengthening it. It certainly will give it a better chance of succeeding. It may make sense to get the other person to agree to speak up for the idea in the meeting—especially if others might expect that person to be in opposition.

- Plan specifically how and when to present your idea or proposal to the team. If possible, use a process that has been agreed upon for the purpose. In most cases, it's helpful to provide team members with a brief outline of your proposal before the meeting, so everyone will have a chance to think through any questions or concerns they want to bring up. It's better to have those out in the open during the meeting rather than to have them come up as "second thoughts" that delay agreement or implementation. Plan ways to involve all team members in the discussion.

- Consider cultural factors that may make a difference to one or more team members. Present your idea in a way that will find a place to land on others' mental map.

Actively Influence

When you bring your proposal, idea, or request to the team, there are several things you can do to give yourself a greater chance of getting their support.

- Let the team know how you plan to proceed, what decision process you expect to follow, and what you are asking of them—you may simply want their agreement for you to take some action or you may need more active support, involvement, or resources from them.

- Be brief, clear, and succinct. In general, giving the headlines and providing support material in written or electronic form is best.

- Begin by showing how your idea or proposal supports the vision of team success. Show how team members, internal or external customers, and the larger organization can benefit. Provide a rationale based on key decision criteria.

- Make time for questions immediately after you first present the idea. You may want to list the questions on a whiteboard (real or virtual) or flip chart before you answer them; in that way you can respond in an order that makes sense to you and keep control of the discussion in your hands.

- Open the discussion to others, especially the opinion leaders you have already influenced to support you.

- If strong objections come up, be open to influence as to how to address them. At all costs, avoid defensiveness. Use receptive behavior to uncover deeper issues.

- Move to a decision once you believe that all major issues have been expressed and responded to.

- If consensus is required and you're not getting it, pose a challenging question—ask what it would take to get the "hold-outs" to support your proposal.

- If you are unable to gain the support of key players during the meeting, postpone the decision and take up the matter with them offline to try to reach a resolution.

Influencing your team requires good planning, timing, and a willingness to use a variety of influence behaviors. It also requires that you be open to being influenced yourself. In order for an entire team to buy in and implement your plan, it has to be perceived as "our plan."

Your Brain on Influence

What Neuroscience and Behavioral Economics Can Teach Us

What lies behind you and what lies in front of you, pales in comparison to what lies inside of you.

—Ralph Waldo Emerson

What Goes on between Our Ears When Someone Tries to Influence Us?

Different parts of our brains are attuned to different situations. Psychologist Drew Westen describes an interesting experiment.* His researchers took MRIs of the brains of people supporting different political candidates as they watched video clips of their candidate contradicting him or herself. When they recognized a contradiction to their own worldview, the "reason and logic" parts of the brain gave way to the parts reserved for "fight-or-flight" responses. Once we've defined a situation as an argument or a fight, with winners and losers, we stop taking in new information. We stop being concerned about who's right and who's wrong

---

*Drew Westen. *The Political Brain* (New York: PublicAffairs, 2008).

and focus on winning. Of course, that very crafty part of our brain is only open to the kind of influence that will help us do that. The minute your target of influence defines you as an adversary, his or her brain won't allow your ideas to be heard.

Because the "fight-or-flight" setting in the brain isn't open to influence, we may need to take some steps to help the other person's brain settle into a place where more rational functions can operate. The FBI's hostage negotiation unit devised a "stairway model" to get a frightened and hostile person to listen to them and take a positive action such as freeing hostages or coming out of hiding and accepting arrest. The model works like this (applying language from our model):

1. Actively listen. Use *Check understanding* to let the other know you've heard him or her.

2. Empathize. Use *Test implications* to express your understanding of their point of view and how they might be feeling.

3. Establish rapport. Use *Identify with other* to show that you empathize (show it, don't just say it) and to build trust.

4. Exercise influence. Once rapport is established, work with them to solve the immediate problem of getting everyone out safely.

This "stairway" is a useful way to approach less drastic but difficult influence situations. Since influence happens between the ears of the other, those ears need to be attuned to new information. The higher functions of the brain don't operate under conditions of perceived threat.

The Power of Cognitive Dissonance

We humans prefer consistency between what we believe and the way we behave, even in retrospect. (If I chose that, it must be because it was right and good.) When we experience a gap, we'll make a strong effort to close it. Leon Festinger, a prominent social psychologist, developed the theory of *cognitive dissonance* in the 1950s. A very old and simple example of this is found in Aesop's fable of the fox and the grapes. When the fox found that it couldn't reach the grapes, it concluded that the grapes must be sour. In other words, if I can't have them, they mustn't be worth much. In his well-received book, *When Prophecy Fails,** Festinger describes what happens when a doomsday cult wakes up to find that the world hasn't ended—and in order to justify their sacrifices (and reduce cognitive

---

*Leon Festinger, Henry Riecken, and Stanley Schachter, *When Prophecy Fails* (Minneapolis, MN: University of Minnesota Press, 1956).

dissonance), they choose to believe that they have saved the world by convincing the aliens not to destroy it.

This very common behavior helps to explain why we have difficulty taking in information that conflicts with strong beliefs or opinions, especially ones we have built our reputation on or spent a lot of resources to obtain or support. Further, this suggests the importance to influencers of spending their energy showing how their idea or request fits with what the other person already values or believes rather than trying to convince the other that he or she is bad, wrong, or stupid.

Why "Homo economicus" Isn't Always a Practical Concept for Influencers

Economic theory since the early nineteenth century has featured the concept of "economic man"—the idea that people make rational choices based on gaining the maximum utility or value at the least cost in money or effort. Recently, however, laboratory research by behavioral economists (social scientists who combine the disciplines of economics and psychology) has shown this to be an unreliable assumption.

Two human tendencies cause us to behave and to make choices that may not, in fact, be in our best interest or that may actually cost us more than they provide in benefits. Those two tendencies are (1) using cognitive biases without being aware of them and (2) relying on habitual mental tools (heuristics) to make decisions. In this chapter, we'll learn about some of them and how to make use of them through influence rather than through manipulation.

We define influence as a conscious act of guiding people toward decisions and actions that are good for us and at the very least not bad for them. We emphasize that it's different from manipulation in that it's done in the open, treats the other with respect, and offers him or her a choice. Working with, rather than against, what's "under the hood" of our decision-making processes can make you a particularly effective influencer—and can also help you to become a better choice maker when you're the one being influenced.

Cognitive Biases and How You Can Make Friends with Them

There are many cognitive biases that survive, usually unexamined, from an earlier time in our individual lives and even in the development of our species when they were probably useful. We've already referred in earlier chapters to the effects of *framing* an idea, offer, or request in language that makes sense and is a good fit for the other's values, goals, and vested interests. This will help you to use *Sell* and *Negotiate* behaviors in a way that will be attractive and meaningful to the other person. We all have biases related to how things should be seen or framed. Let's take a closer look at some of the other common biases that affect decision making. These biases operate below our awareness, but each one provides some insight or application to the way we can influence others.

The Endowment Effect

This is the tendency to overvalue what we already have or to prefer the results of our own labor to that of others. A classic experiment conducted by Daniel Kahneman and Richard Thaler gave some student volunteers coffee mugs and asked them to put a price on them—what they thought the mugs were worth. Other volunteers were asked how much they would pay for such a mug. The "owners" valued the mugs at about twice the amount that others were willing to pay. This tendency has been shown in many experiments with many populations, including with primates other than humans! Because of this tendency to overvalue the results of our own efforts, we develop what behavioral economists call an "adaptive preference" for that which we own or have achieved—even if that means changing our taste. We tend to behave in line with the way we come to see ourselves.

Implications for influence:

The *Encourage* behavior is very helpful in showing others that they have already succeeded in doing something like what you're asking of them now. You remind them of times when they've taken a similar action or mention a quality or skill you've observed in them that aligns with the action. In this way, you can help them to see it as something they already "own." This can create a greater sense of value for the skill or action. Giving honest credit for good work at the time you notice it will make your encouragement that much more powerful when you need to use it. If you only notice in retrospect when you want something from the other, he or she may see the behavior as manipulative—"buttering up."

Loss or Regret Aversion

We hate to lose. In fact, we hate losing about twice as much as we like winning. Amos Tversky and Daniel Kahneman* demonstrated this in their research leading to the development of Prospect Theory, for which Kahneman was awarded a Nobel Prize. This dislike of losing may result in risk and regret aversion. Regret aversion is that voice in your head that says, "If it ain't broke, don't fix it."

---

*Daniel Kahneman and Amos Tversky, "Choices, Values, and Frames," *American Psychologist* 39, no. 4 (1984): 341–350.

"Don't mess with success." "It could get worse." But it also might say, "It's now or never!" as you take your first tandem parachute jump.

Implications for influence:

The behavior *Describe consequences* lets the other know, specifically, what may be lost through a lack of action or a different action from the one you are urging. Often referred to as a "burning platform" (the metaphor, cited by change expert Daryl Conner,* describes a stark choice made by oil rig workers between certain death if they stayed and possible death if they leapt) this behavior can be a strong impetus for individuals and groups to move forward. The behavior is especially useful if people seem stuck or paralyzed into inaction and the consequences they face are real and important.

Social Proof

When uncertain about what to do, we tend to turn to others whom we admire or to whom we ascribe greater knowledge, status, popularity, or political savvy to show us what to do or choose. Websites that rate service providers, restaurants, or films are examples of social proof at work. (If so many people give it five stars, it must be good.) Sometimes this comes in the form of peer pressure, sometimes you simply make the choice to conform rather than venture into the unknown. The "good German" who turned a blind eye to the Holocaust is often used as an example of the negative effects of social proof.

Implications for influence:

It's often useful to garner support or build a coalition before tackling a difficult influence issue. If the person you want to influence doesn't see you as an expert in the relevant area or isn't likely to be impressed by your social or political clout, you can provide greater "social proof" by letting the other know that people he or she respects are in alignment with you on the influence issue. This should be done carefully, without implying that the target of your influence is a slow learner! You may even delegate certain influence tasks to people who are closer to or more admired by your target.

Reciprocity

Reciprocity simply means that like begets like. If someone does a favor for you, you feel a need to "return the favor." We commonly say, "I owe you one." It also works in the opposite way—one bad deed can deserve another. This can lead to an escalating cycle of conflict.

---

*Daryl Conner, *Managing at the Speed of Change: How Resilient Managers Succeed and Prosper Where Others Fail* (New York: Random House, 2006).

Implications for influence:

While "you owe me one" isn't a very effective influence tactic (since we never keep the same "favor books" in our minds), a continuous pattern of offering help or resources when you see they're needed builds a sense of reciprocity with the other.* However, you may need to be explicit about it or the other simply won't notice or remember. Here's where *Offering incentives* can be useful. A quid pro quo offer—even a very simple one—keeps things fair, reduces the possibility of resentment building up over time, and makes future influencing easier. For example, "I'd be happy to take your place in the meeting if you'll give me your notes from the last one." Or, "What do you need from me to make it easier for you to propose my idea to the CEO?" You can also use this insight to avoid getting into an attack-defend cycle. When criticized, use *Inquire* and *Listen* behaviors rather than engaging in tit-for-tat exchanges. This can help maintain an influence relationship that might otherwise melt down.

Confirmation Bias

This refers to our tendency to look for or be swayed by information that confirms our own position. Confirmation bias can cause people to subscribe or listen to one news source (the one that "people like me" pay attention to) rather than expose themselves to a variety of viewpoints. This, of course, leads both to boring dinner parties ("Did you hear the program about . . . of course you did.") and to a more tribal society in which we socialize with people who look like us, do similar work, and vote the same way as we do. This bias also helps explain why people hold onto beliefs that they've invested in even when they're proven to be false. As Festinger pointed out, people who join "doomsday cults" often quit their jobs and sell or give away their belongings to prepare for the end of the world. When the world inconveniently doesn't end, followers most often rationalize this by saying that they had miscalculated the date or that their supplications or sacrifices had saved the world from coming to a crashing halt. Once you have invested in an idea or identified with a cause, you work hard to make sure your commitment was not wasted.

Implications for influence:

Whenever possible, connect your idea, proposal, or request to something the other already believes in. Show him or her areas of agreement and how what you're suggesting can advance the cause. Of course, this only works if you can

---

*Dan Ariely points out the difference between *social* and *market* exchanges. People will willingly do things without payment following a social norm of favor exchange that they would expect to be paid for in the marketplace. In fact, they will do things as a social favor that would otherwise be very costly, where they would be offended by an offer to pay that you could actually afford.

honestly see things through this alternative frame. Using *Inquiring* or *Listening* behaviors will enable you to gain a deeper understanding of the other's point of view, giving you the opportunity to see where you can confirm the other's beliefs with a clear conscience.

Another implication is that you should never waste time trying to prove to someone that he or she is wrong about something if you hope to influence that person. Strong confirmation bias—and the brain operating in a "fight" mode—will fix the other ever more firmly in his or her position. Upselling your idea or solution requires less energy and contains some possibility of influence. However, demanding credit for that same idea may undo all your good influence work! The goal of influencing someone can be at cross-purposes to the very legitimate goal of building your own reputation.

Decision Shortcuts and Their Implications for Influence

We have thousands of decisions to make every day, ranging from what to have for lunch to whom to hire or to marry. It's little wonder that so many of us suffer from "analysis paralysis." Social scientists have pointed out that we often use *heuristics* or rules of thumb in order to simplify decision making. A heuristic is sort of a sloppy algorithm. It suggests a process for finding an answer, not the answer itself. For example, my mother taught me that if ever I was not sure what to do at a dinner party, to observe what the hostess is doing and do the same. That heuristic stood me in very good stead the first time I was confronted with a finger bowl!

Knowing some common heuristics for making decisions can make influencing much easier.

Availability
This shortcut means that whatever is quickly available to one's mind on a particular topic drives decisions. For example, even though airline flights are far safer than other means of transportation, a recent, well-publicized plane crash may cause many people to decide to drive rather than fly to a destination—thus putting more cars on the road and increasing the chances of injury or death while traveling. People typically overestimate the likelihood of dramatic events occurring and underestimate the impact of things that are ordinary and that they feel some control over. Influencers might consider the value of bringing key ideas to the attention of the person they want to influence in a variety of ways over time so that when they begin the active influence process, the idea is easily available to the other's recollection, that is, "Oh, yes, you sent me an article about that just last week."

Representativeness or Familiarity

If we assume that a particular situation is similar to others we're familiar with, we're likely to make a similar choice to the one we made previously. Major consumer companies count on this tendency to create "brand loyalty." In fact, familiar versus unfamiliar situations stimulate different areas of the brain. If we see something as familiar, our frontal and temporal lobes drive us toward using heuristics to make decisions, while in unfamiliar situations, the frontal and parietal lobes operate in a rational, problem-solving mode. When we use *Encourage*, we're reminding the other of a similar action or decision that he or she has taken before, making it easier for him or her to see it as something representative or familiar.

Anchoring

Anchoring is the psychological tendency to fixate on the first piece of information we receive. Many research studies have shown that we tend to cluster our responses to a problem around a number or a topic that the researcher has suggested. The "anchor" affects our choices even though subjects in experiments are typically certain that it has had no effect. In stores, when we see an item marked down from a high price, we believe we're getting a bargain, since we've "anchored" to the higher price. In fact, J.C. Penney's experiment with "everyday low prices" rather than frequent markdowns produced dismal results, since customers had no relevant anchor and thus no sense of the value they had gained. Because of the power of anchoring, we can expect others to be influenced by early suggestions in a conversation as long as those suggestions don't go against their vested interests. It's often useful to make a suggestion or offer early in a negotiation, for example, rather than wait and respond to what the other is asking for. The first offer tends to anchor the conversation around that point.

Affect

Not surprisingly, messages with a stronger emotional component are more persuasive than those that are matter-of-fact. Stories and examples carry much more affect and thus are powerful tools for getting your ideas across. To the degree that people can empathize with the feeling tone of your message, they'll be more likely to take action. Perhaps that's why we say that we're "moved" by a story. Charities understand this and so put a human face on their pitch for our support. When we *Refer to Goals and Benefits*, we can consider using a story or example to illustrate how taking the action can be beneficial. When we *Envision*, we're telling a story about a possible future and our enthusiasm and colorful language provide a positive emotional tone that can be very compelling.

Other Factors at Work in Decision Making

Another important finding related to decision making is the factor of *decision fatigue*. Many studies indicate that we have a limited amount of will power and that if we "spend" it early in the day, there's little left for later decisions. We refuse the doughnuts in the office kitchen, but order dessert at dinner. We run for an hour in the morning, but then have trouble getting around to studying for a test later in the day. We make wise decisions in our role as a leader but then get caught by the media doing foolish things after hours.

The number of choices can also cause paralysis. Research by Iyengar and Lepper* found that "people who had more choices were often less willing to decide to buy anything at all. . . ." Giving people two or three strong reasons or options to consider (informed by what they find useful, interesting, or of value) rather than overwhelming them with data is usually the more effective expressive influence approach.

The reciprocal of influence is decision-making. While we'd prefer to see ourselves and our colleagues, friends, and families as primarily rational beings, we'll be less successful influencers and poorer decision makers if we don't recognize that our bodies—especially our brains—are wired to make certain choices below our awareness. Knowing this, we can recognize that great ideas don't sell themselves, that rational arguments can be perfectly formulated without actually moving anyone to action. We can take time to deconstruct our own decisions to see if they actually accord with what's right and best for us and for those close to us—or if we've made them "on automatic." We can give people time enough to think about their decisions so that they can truly consider the options rather than living with regret or choosing to avoid making a commitment.

---

*S. Iyengar and M. Lepper, "When Choice Is Demotivating: Can One Desire Too Much of a Good Thing?" *Journal of Personal and Social Psychology* 79, no. 6 (December, 2000): 995–1006.

The Paradox of Failure

Every moment instructs, and every object: for wisdom is infused into every form.
—Ralph Waldo Emerson

Win Some, Lose Some, Learn Some

So . . . you set your goal, did your homework, got the support you needed, planned, and executed. And you failed. You didn't influence the other person after all that. Your daughter still went off to Europe alone. The boss wouldn't approve your project. The recalcitrant committee members gave a minority report. How do you deal with it?

First, sit down and have a nice cup of tea. Call a friend. Rant and rave. Or, if you prefer, read a trashy novel, or watch an old movie with a lot of car crashes in it. Get used to it, though, because once you start being conscious about influencing, you will notice that you fail a lot. Of course, this is because you are paying attention rather than doing the blindfolded drive-by influencing you used to prefer. You are failing because you're taking risks—and it is the nature of risk to be associated with failure as much as with success.

But after you get past the first twenty minutes or so of teeth gnashing, you will acknowledge that you have, after all, had partial successes, and here and there a really glorious moment. And you'll probably notice also that you have learned a lot from the things that didn't work, and that you feel more in charge of your own life than you used to. Being the persistent person you are, you will continue to try to shape the events that make your world. You will develop a better sense of humor. And you will live to influence another day. Here is one last favorite Emerson quote:

"All promise outruns the performance. We live in a system of approximations. Every end is prospective of some other end, which is also temporary; a round and final success nowhere. We are encamped in nature, not domesticated."

What? So What? Now What?

That about sums up the way to treat your influence experiences. If what you're doing isn't working, you can stop doing it. You would probably rather not reproduce the same mistakes. (To quote George Santayana, "Those who cannot learn from the past will be condemned to repeat it.") You will probably want to remember what worked well, so you can do it again. It's worth your while to take some time to reflect about an influence opportunity just after it's over. A quick formula for this is to use the questions: What? So what? Now what? What happened, what does it mean, and what am I going to do about it?

Then download or pick up that novel and head for the beach.

APPENDIX

A

Coaching Partnerships

The most effective way to learn and improve your influence skills is to work with a trusted partner who will encourage you to practice them and will give you honest feedback and coaching. The ideal coaching partner for learning influence skills is a person who also wishes to improve his or her skills, but is different from you in some important ways. Some of those differences could include

- Communication and influence skills and abilities
- Role
- Profession
- Goals and vested interests

The differences are important because they will enable you to provide objective feedback to one another and to have a richer set of experiences and skills to draw from. At the same time, you need to have a set of shared values and a shared commitment to learning and improving. A high degree of mutual trust is a prerequisite to working together in this way.

Coaching sessions can take place in person or virtually. If virtual, it's best to use a video-based communication medium so that you can give and receive feedback on nonverbal as well as verbal aspects of your practice.

You and your coaching partner will begin with an initial session to establish goals and plan for subsequent sessions. Ideally, each of you will have completed the first section of this book. During the first meeting, which may take an hour or so, you should try to do most of the following activities. Make sure you leave time for both of you to complete each activity.

1. Do the Sphere of Influence (Figure 2.1) exercise together and discuss it.
2. Identify typical influence situations that occur in your lives.
3. Share some longer-term goals you would like to achieve that will require improved influencing skills.
4. Decide on one or two areas in which you would like to focus your practice at first. These should be actions that you believe you should do more often or more effectively in order to achieve your goals.
5. Select an upcoming influence opportunity that you can prepare for in the next session.
6. Set a time for your next session.

In subsequent meetings, you may want to do some of the following activities:

1. Prepare for an upcoming influence opportunity by using the Influence Plan in Appendix B and consulting with your partner.
   - Set a goal.
   - Develop the influence framework.
   - Choose the most useful behaviors.
   - Practice the scenario with your partner. Ask him or her to take the role of the person you're hoping to influence.
   - Stop and start the scenario every two or three minutes to obtain feedback from your partner as to whether you are moving closer to your goal. Ask for suggestions about what might work better.
   - Try it in several different ways by asking your partner to respond differently and/or by trying different behaviors.
2. Choose a specific behavior to practice and have your partner suggest situations that you might use for practice. For example, suppose you want to practice a *Listen* behavior such as *Check understanding.* Your partner might launch the following scenarios:
   - Your manager has just told you that you can't go to a seminar you had been planning on attending.
   - Your colleague has canceled a standing meeting for the third time without explanation.
   - Your teenage son or daughter has informed you that a friend has offered hang-gliding lessons.

3. Your partner will respond as if he or she were the person you are influencing. Whatever he or she says, you will respond by using the *Listen* behavior you chose to practice. Stop after a few minutes and ask your partner what was going on. Did he or she become more or less open to influence through the process? What worked well about the way you responded? What could be improved? Try the same situations with a different behavior. Focus more on practicing the behavior than on achieving the goal.

4. Identify opportunities to practice this specific skill in the real world before your next meeting, and commit to debriefing your experiences with your partner.

Influence Plan

Part 1

Following is a series of questions that fall within each of the areas of the influence framework. Some, but not all, of the questions will be appropriate to the situation you're thinking about. Review the questions in each area and highlight the ones that you believe to be relevant to the outcome of your influence opportunity. Answer the key questions, then think of how you will use the information to build the relationship, and achieve your desired results.

Results

- What is your vision of success? What role will the other person play in it?
- What are the needs that underlie your vision? For you? For the organization? For the person you are influencing?
- What specific long-term and short-term goals do you have for the influence opportunity?
- What are your criteria for success? How will you know you have achieved the results you are aiming for?
- What alternative outcomes might satisfy your underlying needs and achieve equivalent results?

Relationship

- What is the history of your (or your team's) influence relationship (in both directions) with this person or group?
- What is the current level of trust? Why? What can you do to increase it?
- What assumptions do each of you hold about the other? How will you test them? How might they affect the outcome?

- What is the power balance between you?
- What are the current or continuing issues in the relationship, regardless of whether they are directly related to this influence opportunity?
- How important might this influence relationship be or become in the future?

Context

Individual

- What are the relevant values of the other? How are they similar or different from yours?
- What are his or her high-priority goals right now? Yours?
- What common or conflicting vested interests are important in this situation? What does each of you have to gain or lose?
- What are the important current issues that have an impact on this person?
- How would you describe his or her communication or work style? How does he or she generally prefer to be approached? How does your usual approach match with his or her preferences? How might you want to modify it?

Organizational

- How does the business strategy of the organization relate to the subject at hand? Are the results you envision a good fit for the organizational strategy and goals?
- How will the organization's structure and processes affect your influence approach? Is your approach out of the norm?
- Where does this issue stand in the ranking of organizational priorities?
- How might the formal or informal power structure in the organization affect the outcome of your influence action?
- Who are other stakeholders in the outcome of your action? How will you involve them?

Cultural

- What are the cultural values (organizational, professional, national, or ethnic) that are relevant to this issue?
- What are the norms (formal or informal ground rules) that you should be aware of?
- What are some of the cultural assumptions that relate to this situation?

- What are the usual cultural practices or rituals that might be useful in this situation?
- Are there any cultural taboos that could derail your approach?

External

- What trends, issues, or events are going on right now in the larger systems you are a part of? How might they have an impact on your influence opportunity?

Approach

- Given your analysis of the situation, what do you intend for your influence behaviors to achieve?
- What are the best specific behaviors to achieve those results?

Part 2

Once you've reviewed the list of questions, proceed with your plan as follows:

1. Highlight the key questions that you want to explore.
2. Summarize the results on the Influence Framework (see Figure 3.1).
3. Focus and refine your influence goal, using the FOCUS criteria in Figure 8.1.
4. Consider the issues that may be raised for the other person by your suggestion, request, or offer.
5. Identify the tactics that would be most appropriate for working with these issues.
6. Choose the most applicable behaviors, which may be different from what you originally thought. Refer to Tables 14.1 and 14.2 for guidance.
7. Plan a sequence. You might develop a few different options, depending on the other's response. Influencing is a nonlinear, yet goal-focused, process!
8. Troubleshoot. Ask yourself, "What might go wrong with this plan?" Then think of ways to course-correct.
9. Focus on your next steps. Influence is a process, not an event.
10. Evaluate and learn. Ask for feedback on your plan from someone you trust, rehearse it if possible—then upgrade. After you've implemented the plan, take a few minutes to reflect on what worked, what didn't, what you've learned, how you can apply it, and next steps with the person or group you're influencing.

Meeting Processes That Support Effective Influencing

We Have to Start Meeting Like This

Since so much influencing takes place at formal or informal meetings (virtual or face-to-face) at work, at home, or in your community, following are some suggestions for designing meetings for effective two-way influencing. If the outcome of the meeting is to be a decision or set of actions that will require the commitment of participants, it's especially important that each person have an opportunity to influence the end result. Too many meetings are designed to avoid engaging people in discussion about decisions that they will have to buy into and implement. This only lengthens the overall process.

1. If you are the person calling the meeting, spend some one-on-one time conferring with other key stakeholders (those who have something to gain or lose by the outcome of the meeting) and get their ideas as to what should be on the agenda, who should be invited, time—or time zone—place, and other details.

2. Send out the agenda or let participants know in advance the topics that will be discussed. That way, those who like to think before they speak out (mainly the introverts among us—whose thoughtful comments may be lost

otherwise) will have a chance to prepare to influence others at the meeting. This tends to increase engagement and shorten the meeting, because people will come prepared. In addition, establishing topics in advance can prevent the situation that arises when someone who did not participate actively at the last meeting now wants to re-open the topic for discussion, just when you thought the matter was settled.

3. Ask someone to facilitate the meeting. This is especially important if there will be difficult or controversial topics on the agenda, or if the group typically tends to become bogged down in details or get sidetracked. The person who is facilitating should be someone without a vested interest in the outcome of the issues under discussion. This can be a rotating role in your group, or you can use someone outside the group who has had some training in meeting facilitation. The job of the facilitator is to manage the process of the meeting by agreement with other members of the group. He or she should not contribute to the content without publicly stepping out of his or her facilitator role. See the Resources section for suggestions.

4. State clearly in the agenda, and again at the beginning of the meeting, the purpose of the session and the process you will follow. It's helpful for participants to know what results are expected. Which of the following best describes your purpose?

   • Communicate information.

   • Gather information.

   • Explore problems or issues.

   • Make a decision.

   • Announce a decision and discuss how to implement it.

5. Establish a set of norms or ground rules for this meeting (or to use at all meetings of a particular group) that will ensure that everyone has a fair chance to be heard and to influence the decisions appropriately. Ask participants for suggestions and then be sure to enforce them in a good-natured way. Some examples might be

   • Have a time limit for each person's comments on a particular topic.

   • Ask for someone's ideas if he or she has not spoken for a while.

   • Ask the group for alternatives before settling on a solution.

6. In meetings that are primarily expressive in nature (such as meetings that communicate information or decisions), it's important to set aside time afterward to use receptive skills to gather questions and/or listen to concerns.

7. In meetings that are primarily receptive in nature (such as meetings that are held for the purpose of gathering information or exploring

issues), it's important to begin with an expressive statement informing or reminding participants of the purpose and process and why they are being involved. It may also be useful to share a vision of the ideal results of the meeting and encourage participants to be active and open.

8. Overall, meetings should be designed to enable participants to move back and forth between expressing their ideas and learning about what others think. There is little chance of a successful result if everyone is only interested in expressing his or her ideas—or, for that matter, if no one is willing to take the risk of putting an idea on the table. A good facilitator can be very helpful with this.

9. Use different processes during the meeting to involve everyone who has something to contribute. For example, try a "nominal group process" in which each person contributes a thought or idea, one at a time. (There should always be an option to pass and the process should continue for several rounds, allowing new ideas to develop and for participants to be willing to put them forward.)

10. Be sure to separate processes that are meant to generate ideas, such as brainstorming, from processes that are evaluative and meant to move toward decision making. Use ground rules that support the process you are using. (For example, brainstorming processes require a "no evaluation of ideas" ground rule to be successful.)

11. Notice when someone who is key to implementing the group's decision, or whose support is important, is not participating or is giving signals that he or she is not happy with the direction. This may be difficult to ascertain during virtual meetings, so the leader or facilitator should check in with key people from time to time (i.e., "William, what are your thoughts about this?"). Use receptive skills to invite that person to participate and/or to express concerns.

12. For important decisions that require participants' support, consider using a consensus process. Consensus does not mean that everyone believes it is the best possible decision—it means that everyone has agreed that he or she can live with, support, and implement the decision. A consensus decision process involves

    • A proposal for a decision, often a summary of a discussion about the issues involved

    • A question: "Who can't support the decision as stated?"

    • A query to those who are not in agreement: "What would have to change in order for you to be able to live with and implement the decision?"

- A discussion and good-faith effort to modify the decision to gain the support of those who disagree
- Another check for agreement

This process may be repeated several times until a consensus is reached.

13. If your meetings are typified by "groupthink," where people tend to cluster around similar ideas or come to agreement without challenging one another, ask someone to act as "devil's advocate" for any important decision, questioning assumptions or rationale and asking for alternatives.

14. Consider who, outside of the group, will need to be influenced in order for any meeting decisions to be implemented successfully. Discuss how to approach the influence tasks as next steps in the decision process.

Influencing in Global and Virtual Teams

All of the suggestions above are valid, whether the meeting is held face-to-face or by video, telephone, or web conference. When participants in the meeting are not co-located, special care should be taken to make sure that everyone has an opportunity to participate and influence. From time to time, the facilitator or leader in a virtual meeting should do a "round-robin" check for comments, opinions, or questions from each participant by name (always allowing for a "pass" response).

Virtual meetings that involve global teams have special issues. Time zones could shift from one meeting to another—possible because of who is hosting the meeting, but also to be fair about sharing the difficulty of meeting outside of regular working hours equitably. Seemingly simple issues like this can have an impact on where people believe power resides and can have an effect on a member's perceived ability to influence the team.

When possible, global teams should have an occasional face-to-face meeting, or at least a video meeting so that members have a more personal sense of one another. This, too, increases the likelihood of active influencing across boundaries of time and space.

Cultural differences about influence can have an important impact on global teams. For example, some cultures are more hierarchical than others, causing younger, newer, or less senior members to withhold their ideas—which can be a real loss. Any team leader or manager will do well to learn about these cultural differences that can be barriers to communication and influence so that he or she can find appropriate ways (through team norms, for example) to encourage full participation. Teams and organizations with a healthy climate for influence can be more focused, aligned, and innovative—they can trust the agreements they reach and know that good ideas will be shared.

D

Sentence Starters

Expressive Behaviors

Tell

"I recommend that..."

"I suggest that we..."

"It's important to me that..."

"I need..."

Sell

"My analysis shows..."

"The reasons are..."

"This could help us achieve..."

"The benefits would be..."

Negotiate

"If you will do this, I will..."

"In exchange, I'll..."

"Here's what I can do to make it work..."

"I need to let you know the consequences of..."

Enlist

"Here's what I believe could happen..."

"I can see us..."

"As a team, we can ... "
"I know you are capable of ... "

Receptive Behaviors

Inquire

"What do you think about ... ?"
"What ideas do you have for ... ?"
"Help me understand ... "
"Tell me more about ... "

Listen

"So from your point of view ... "
"Your problem with this is ... "
"I'm wondering if you're concerned about ... "
"You seem hesitant. Could that be because ... ?"

Attune

"I know how busy you are these days ... "
"If I were in your shoes, I might want ... "
"You're right. I should have ... "
"I really need help on ... "

Facilitate

"So your dilemma is ... "
"On the one hand ... and on the other ... ."
"What would it take for you to ... ?"
"How might you go about doing that?"

Influence Scenarios

Let's revisit the scenarios from the beginning of the book. In the following few pages, we'll imagine a better (though not necessarily ideal—that's life!) outcome for each scenario through the conscious use of influence. As you read the scenarios, notice which behavioral skills are being used and how some of the principles discussed in the book are being implemented. These are not intended as "school solutions" to these problems. Rather, they represent one productive way to approach the situation. How might you handle the situations now that you've had a chance to think about the process of influence?

1. It's five o'clock. You've been at your desk since six this morning, and you're nowhere near ready to go home. You have a meeting with your manager tomorrow morning, and you're supposed to have a report finished. You would have, too, if the other people involved had done their parts. First, the data was late from your counterpart in the other group. The people on your team had other priorities and couldn't help you with the analysis. Then the "admin" was too busy to help you prepare a decent-looking presentation. You might have asked your manager for an extension, but you didn't want to look unprepared, so you decided to do it all yourself. It looks like an all-nighter.

It's two weeks before your report is due. You notice that some of the data you are waiting for is overdue from your counterpart in the other group. You call and arrange to meet him briefly in the cafeteria. Your goal is to obtain a commitment from him to give you the information that you need. Over coffee, you have the following conversation:

> You: *Kumar, I'm aware that you haven't given the data to me this week, as you had agreed. What's holding it up?*
>
> Kumar: *Yes, I know. I thought I could, but I've run into a problem.*
>
> You: *Tell me about the problem.*

Kumar: *Well, the analyst who started it fell while skiing and ended up with a concussion. I don't really have anyone else who can do this kind of work. He won't be back for at least a week.*

You: *How far did he get before he left for the ski trip?*

Kumar: *He had worked out the major conclusions, but had just started the detailed report.*

You: *That helps. If you can give me the work he did, I'll use the "headlines" in my report. If my manager wants the detail, we'll have time to work it out. In a pinch, could you work on it? I'd be willing to cover you for your team meetings if you can put in enough time to give my boss something she can live with—only if she asks for it, of course.*

Kumar: *That gives me some breathing room. I appreciate the offer, I was uncomfortable that I was letting you down.*

You: *Thanks. I'd like the report, as it is, later today. I'll let you know if and when we need the supportive data.*

2. Your teenage daughter, a bright and successful student, has announced that she will be turning down a scholarship to a prestigious university in favor of taking a year off to travel and "find herself." You've had several heated arguments about this. Recently, you told her that you couldn't guarantee that you would pay her college tuition when she returned. Her response was that she was perfectly capable of earning her own money and attending a less expensive school. You feel that you've painted yourself into a corner and haven't made any progress in convincing her of the importance to her future of making the right college choice. You're also concerned about her safety as a solo traveler in certain parts of the world.

You suspect that the approach you've been taking with your daughter has polarized both of you on the issue. You decide to take a fresh approach. You invite her out to lunch and begin a conversation with her. Your goal is to get her to agree to reconsider her plans.

You: *I believe I've been pretty unproductive in the way I've talked with you about your plans. I was thinking that, if I were in your shoes, I'd probably be more convinced than ever that I needed to make an independent decision about it.*

Daughter: *I'm not trying to go against what you say. I just believe that I need to take time out from going to school right now. It's been a pretty intense year, and I need a break.*

You: *Help me understand what this trip would mean for you.*

Daughter: *I just want some time to figure out what I want to do. I feel as if I've been meeting everyone else's expectations for a long time, and I'm not sure any more that I want to do the things that other people want for me.*

You: *So you want a little time and space to get to know yourself away from parents and teachers . . .*

Daughter: *Exactly.*

You: *What are some options for making that happen in addition to the solo trip you've been thinking about?*

Daughter: *I might be able to talk Sarah into going with me . . .*

You: *What else might work?*

Daughter: *I'm not sure . . .*

You: *I know that the community college offers some small group tours for young people. Would that be an option?*

Daughter: *It would depend. I'm not interested in "if it's Tuesday, it must be Paris" kind of tours.*

You: *Another possibility might be to opt for the "Sophomore Year Abroad" program at the school that wants you . . .*

Daughter: *I did like the sound of that.*

You: *Would you consider trying the school for a year, preparing for that year abroad? If you would do that, I'd be willing to pay for a summer trip with a group this year, as long as you and I can agree on one that's reputable and affordable.*

Daughter: *I will think it over. It sounds pretty good, but I need to make my own decision about it.*

You: *I trust you to do that. It's hard for me to let go, but you really are an adult now. Let's talk about it later in the week.*

3. You are a senior executive charged with the responsibility for implementing the final steps in merging two companies. Executives of the other firm, who see this as an acquisition by your company rather than a merger, are dragging their feet in regard to getting their systems aligned with yours. They give you excuses that sound rational, but the net effect is to delay the implementation. You're under a lot of pressure to get this completed. The new, merged systems should have been up and running by now, and you're feeling very frustrated and angry.

You've decided to meet with your counterpart from the other company to see whether you can enlist her help in merging the systems. You set a time and meet her at her office.

You: *Thanks for meeting with me, Heather. I'd like to talk about some issues regarding merging our HR and information systems.*

Heather: *Well, I'm really quite busy, so I can't take more than a few minutes today.*

You: *Heather, I really need your help on this. I'm puzzled about how to proceed. I don't seem to be getting very far. What do you think is holding the process up?*

Heather: *Well, everyone is so busy, with the merger and all . . .*

You: *Heather, I know how busy all of you are. Frankly, I'm concerned that we won't be ready by the time the merger is set to be final. I will personally have to go to the CEO next week and tell him that we're not on track, and I'm not looking forward to that meeting. I expect him to be pretty upset, and I would imagine that we will all feel the brunt of that. At least I know I will. So that's why I would like your help. I'm thinking that people may be concerned about learning the new systems. Could that be the issue?*

Heather: *I don't really think that's it. Everyone on the leadership team is committed to making this work. The problem is, we got everyone in the company involved in designing and implementing our current system. It took a lot of time. They were really committed to it. And now they see this new one as being imposed on them. We're getting a lot of resistance from some of our best people. They see it as a sign that this is an acquisition, not a merger. They're putting their resumes out on the web. It's all we can do to get through the day without a crisis. You know, people really put their hearts and souls into growing this company.*

You: *So you're concerned about losing good people if they see that their commitment and loyalty may not be repaid.*

Heather: *Yes. They're pretty demoralized.*

You: *Do you have any ideas about what might help?*

Heather: *I think it might help if they knew that nobody would be downsized. Your company has committed to that, but they don't trust the words.*

You: *What if we put together a committee from both companies to start the process of merging the info system? You could include the informal leaders of the company, and it would be a way for them to get to know their counterparts.*

Heather: *That might be good, although they may not be very enthusiastic about volunteering.*

You: *Are you thinking that they might worry about appearing to be "co-opted" by the big guys?*

Heather: *You've got it.*

You: *Here's my suggestion. Let's put together an all-hands meeting for both companies. We can lead it together and invite questions and concerns from the audience.*

I think that our attitude might well help resolve some of their concerns. We could then ask for volunteers to serve on the committee.

Heather: *That sounds like a reasonable way to go . . .*

4. You volunteered to help plan and host the yearly fund-raiser for your child's preschool. You were reluctant to take this on for fear that you might end up, as has happened before, doing it all yourself. The first few meetings of your committee were very positive; several people volunteered to take responsibility for specific tasks. Now it's two weeks before the event, and several important things haven't happened. Everyone has an excuse for not delivering on his or her commitments. You feel that the staff and board are depending on you, and you don't want to let them down. This experience has convinced you, however, that you're not cut out for community leadership. You feel burned out and disappointed.

You're determined to get some help to pull this event off. You decide to call one of the committee members and see what you can do to get him or her to recommit.

You: *Hello, Chris. I'm glad I reached you. I need to talk with you about the fund-raiser.*

Chris: *I'm so sorry that I haven't been able to come through on that. I've been completely swamped at work. I just didn't anticipate that, and I feel bad about it. In fact, I'm embarrassed.*

You: *I know that you really want to help. You've been a real supporter of the school, and I believe that you're completely committed to making this a success.*

Chris: *Yes, but I just can't do what I originally promised.*

You: *Here's what's going on for me. The catering decisions and the follow-up calls to the presenters are really overdue. I'm afraid that we'll get to the day and find that we have no food and no speakers. There are several other things that I'm trying to do after work, but frankly, if I don't have help, some things won't be done, and we'll all be really disappointed. And I'm going to have a lot of egg on my face as the chair. . . . Chris, what would it take for you to take on one of those tasks?*

Chris: *If you can give me the speakers' phone numbers or e-mail addresses, I'll take on the task of preparing them. I didn't realize that we were so far behind.*

You: *Thanks, that will help a lot.*

5. You've been nurturing an idea for a couple of years now. It would be an application of your current technology that you believe would have a tremendous impact on the market. It would require a moderate commitment of resources, but the payoff could be spectacular. The problem is that such a project is outside of your current area of responsibility and, in fact, might be seen as competitive with another team's current project. Your manager has already told you that you would have to have it approved and funded elsewhere. You're beginning to suspect that it's a political "hot potato." You're still hoping that someone will recognize the potential and support it, but you feel discouraged.

You decide to go, with your manager's approval, to the senior manager who is accountable for both groups. Your goal is to influence her to agree to sponsor the idea and provide funding. You've asked your manager to set up the meeting and you're well prepared. You just finished explaining the proposal to her.

You: *What questions do you have about my proposal?*

Barbara: *How do you suggest funding the project? We don't have any budget for something like this.*

You: *In my proposal, I talked about some ways to minimize costs by sharing facilities with another project. I believe that the project will more than pay for itself within two years. Given the need we've been hearing for diversifying our product line, this could look good to the board. What could I do that would convince you to take this on?*

Barbara: *I do like the idea. I might be willing to bring it up at the next executive committee meeting to see whether we might find some special funding for it. That would be very difficult, though. Can you create a ten-minute presentation that summarizes benefits and costs? I would be willing to bring it up if I have something to show them.*

You: *I'll get it to you by the end of the week. Let me know if I can help you prepare.*

6. You were recently offered an exciting new position with your company. It would involve spending three years abroad and would probably lead to a significant role for you in the company's future. When you told your spouse about it, you expected enthusiastic support. Instead, you received a flat and resistant response. This surprised you, as you have always agreed that whichever one of you was offered the best opportunity would have the other's support, regardless of any inconvenience and disruption that might occur.

You've just learned that your spouse is highly resistant to moving abroad, which will be required if you are to accept the new position. You expressed a lot of surprise and anger. Now you think that you'd better pick yourself up, dust yourself off, and begin to explore the issues. Your goal is to influence your spouse to agree to consider the matter and give it a fair hearing, rather than refuse right away.

> You: *I really overreacted just then. I was truly surprised by your refusal, and I didn't respond very well. I need to listen to your concerns. What kind of problems would this create for you?*
>
> Spouse: *Well, in the first place, I'm at a really critical place in my project right now, and it would be career limiting to leave in the middle of it. And I don't like the idea of moving the kids out of their school. It's been very hard to find a school that works well for both of them.*
>
> You: *So there are two main issues: What would happen to your career and how the kids would cope with another new school?*
>
> Spouse: *Yes. I know we agreed to trade off on this, but that was before we were really settled and had a family. The situation is different now.*
>
> You: *And specifically, that's mainly because we have kids, as you see it . . .*
>
> Spouse: *And because we both are pretty committed to our current jobs.*
>
> You: *What do you see as the options we have now?*
>
> Spouse: *One possibility might be to see whether you could start by working from here and going over once a month or so. That would be the least disruptive.*
>
> You: *What else might work?*
>
> Spouse: *Well, I can see that I'll have more flexibility in about six months. I could think about a short-term move. But only if we could make it work for the kids.*
>
> You: *So your suggestion is that I see whether I can get them to agree to a start-up period where I'd be based here. If I do that, you'd be willing to consider a later move.*
>
> Spouse: *Yes. I really need to have some time to get used to the idea, of course. And to do some research on schools and possible jobs for me. I do want to keep our agreement, but I'm just not ready to make a complete commitment.*
>
> You: *I really appreciate you working this through with me. I'm pretty optimistic that we can work something out, if I can get my manager to be flexible.*

7. You lead an important project for your company. The project is not going as well as you had hoped. There's a lot of conflict, and milestones are not being achieved. You were selected for this role because of your technical skills, but you're feeling dragged down by the day-to-day hassle of dealing with people's egos and

working out the turf issues that seem to get in the way of every cross-functional team you have worked with.

You decide to meet with a key member of your team, Terry. Your goal is to influence him to agree to help you with the "people issues" on the team.

> You: *Thanks for taking the time to meet with me. I'll get right to the point and tell you that I need some advice from you. You seem to me to have a lot of success in getting your group to work together. Your people skills have always impressed me. I'd like to see our whole team operating as well together as your part of the team does. I could really use your help in getting past the "turf issues" that are getting in our way.*
>
> Terry: *I do have a group that works well together. I'm not sure that has much to do with me. . . .*
>
> You: *Terry, I see you as a real catalyst for that. You seem to know how to keep people aligned toward a common goal. I can imagine how effective we could be as a team if everyone were focused on the overall goal, and I can see you as key to making that happen.*
>
> Terry: *Well, I'm willing to work with you, but as a peer, I'm pretty limited in what I can say or do. I think it will require a change in process as well as a change in attitude.*
>
> You: *You sound concerned that people will think you're taking on too broad a role. Is that it?*
>
> Terry: *Yes, I don't want to limit my effectiveness by looking like I'm angling for a bigger role.*
>
> You: *What if you were to help me plan a team meeting? My meetings are usually pretty technical. I'm not experienced in looking at team process. They don't teach you how to do that in engineering school. Would you be willing to do that?*
>
> Terry: *Sure. I'll help you plan a meeting as long as you're clearly in charge of it.*
>
> You: *I'll be very clear that it's my meeting. In exchange, would you be willing to facilitate it?*
>
> Terry: *Sure, I can do that.*

8. You chair a standards task force for your association that could have a major impact on the conduct of your profession. Some members of the group are very resistant to the idea of mandatory compliance with the standards. You and several others believe that it's an exercise in futility to develop and present standards and then let people choose whether to adopt them or not. The differences have

divided the group, which has now reached an impasse. If you can't come to an agreement, the entire exercise will be seen as a waste of time. You're concerned that you might lose the respect of your colleagues, both within the task force and outside of it. They've been counting on you to resolve this issue.

You decide to begin the next meeting by confronting the issue in a way that you hope will be productive. Your goal is to influence a key colleague to reconsider his or her opposition.

> You: *I want to acknowledge the good news about what we've done so far. I think I haven't been appreciative enough that we've been able to reach agreement on professional standards. That's really quite an accomplishment, and everyone has worked hard to make it happen. I'm hoping that by the end of the meeting today, we'll be a lot closer to agreement about how to implement those standards. I'd like to start by asking those of you who've been supporting the idea of voluntary compliance to say what your major concern is about making them mandatory.*
>
> Colleague: *We've been through all that. Mainly, the issue is that our professional values are really opposed to coercion, and mandatory standards would seem very bureaucratic to the members. Also, I think that there are some very good people in the profession whose training wouldn't come up to the standards we're recommending.*
>
> You: *So you're concerned that some key people would not meet the standards.*
>
> Colleague: *Yes, but the coercion issue is also important.*
>
> You: *What could we do that would make it possible for you to support a stricter implementation of the standard? How could we modify it so you could live with it?*
>
> Colleague: *Clearly, we'd have to have a "grandfather and grandmother" rule: Anyone who's been in the society for more than a few years wouldn't have to meet the standards.*
>
> You: *What else could we do that would make it possible for you to support enforcing the standards?*
>
> Colleague: *I'm not sure. . . .*
>
> You: *What if we were to open up the process—to have the standards approved by most of the membership and to agree to a review after two years?*
>
> Colleague: *That would begin to meet some of my concerns . . .*

F

Self-Assessment

Instructions: Rate yourself on the following influence behaviors. This rating will provide valuable information to you in developing a mutually beneficial influence relationship with your colleagues. Use the following rating scale and record your response in the box to the right of the question, then note where you would like to focus your practice.

- -

N/A = Not applicable. (Not appropriate or needed in the situations you face.)

⬆ = I could do this more often. (If I used this behavior more, I would exercise influence more effectively.)

✓ = I do this about as often as I would like. (I am satisfied with the frequency with which I use this behavior.)

⬇ = I could do this less often. (I use this behavior more frequently than is appropriate.)

✱ = I do this differently from the way I would prefer. (For example, I may give reasons in the appropriate situations, but if I chose reasons that were more convincing to the other person, it would be more effective.)

You may wish to use more than one symbol. For example, you may use a behavior less often than you would like *and* you want to do it differently. You would then mark ⬆ and ✱ in the box.

1. Offer useful suggestions .... ☐
2. Express needs directly.. ☐
3. Support my proposals with good reasons .... ☐
4. Show others how my proposal fits in with what they believe .... ☐
5. Willing to offer a fair exchange when asking something of others........................ ☐
6. Let others know of any realistic consequences to them in taking or not taking an action.......... ☐
7. Help others to see a clear vision of success at the end of the road I would like them to take ..... ☐
8. Show others that I believe in their ability to achieve the vision.......................... ☐
9. Ask thought-provoking questions .... ☐
10. Explore information and ideas, don't just take things at face value .... ☐
11. Paraphrase what others have said and check my understanding .... ☐
12. Test the meaning behind what the other person is saying by making an educated guess........ ☐
13. Find and comment on areas of mutual concern or interest................................... ☐
14. Be open about my motivation.. ☐
15. Summarize the issues and concerns that the other person is facing .... ☐
16. Challenge others to take action and responsibility.. ☐

Enter your ratings in the boxes corresponding to the number of the question. Then use the chart below to identify the behaviors and note which ones you may wish to develop or improve.

Self Assessment:
Results

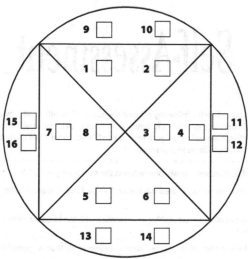

Notes:

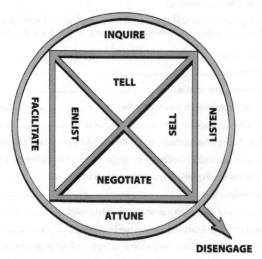

RESOURCES

Workshops and Seminars

Constructive Debate: Building Better Ideas. Barnes & Conti Associates, Inc., 510.644.0911, www.barnesconti.com.

Constructive Negotiation: Building Agreements That Work. Barnes & Conti Associates, Inc., 510.644.0911, www.barnesconti.com.

Exercising Influence: Building Relationships and Getting Results. Barnes & Conti Associates, Inc., 510.644.0911, www.barnesconti.com.

Facilitating Forward: Guiding Others Toward Results. Barnes & Conti Associates, Inc., 510.644.0911, www.barnesconti.com.

Facilitative Leadership (for meetings). Interaction Associates, Inc., Tel. +1-617-535-7000 or +1-415-343-2600, www.interactionassociates.com.

Inspirational Leadership: Encouraging Others to Do Great Things. Barnes & Conti Associates, Inc., 510.644.0911, www.barnesconti.com.

Principles of Graphic Facilitation (for meetings). The Grove Consultants, Inc., 800.494.7683, www.grove.com.

Instrument

Myers-Briggs Type Indicator. Consulting Psychologists Press, Inc., https://www.cpp.com/en/index.aspx, www.mbti.com.

Additional Reading

Ariely, Dan. *Predictably Irrational: The Hidden Forces That Shape Our Decisions.* New York: Harper Perennial, 2011.

Chabris, Christopher, and David Simons. *The Invisible Gorilla: How Our Intuitions Deceive Us.* New York: Crown, 2010.

Cialdini, Robert B. Influence: The Psychology of Persuasion, *Rev. Ed.* New York: Harper Business, 2006.

Emerson, Ralph Waldo. *Self-reliance*. Belton, TX: Seahorse Publishing, 2013.

Festinger, Leon, Henry Riecken, and Stanley Schachter. *When Prophecy Fails*. Kindle Edition. New York: Start Publishing, 2013.

Fisher, Roger, and Alan Sharp. *Getting It Done: How to Lead When You Are Not in Charge*. New York: HarperCollins, 1998.

Gladwell, Malcolm. *The Tipping Point: How Little Things Can Make A Big Difference*. Boston: Little Brown, 2000.

Goleman, Daniel. *Working with Emotional Intelligence*. New York: Bantam Books, 1998.

Hogan, Kevin. *The Psychology of Persuasion: How to Persuade Others to Your Way of Thinking*. Gretna, LA: Pelican Publishing, 2004.

Kahneman, Daniel. *Thinking, Fast and Slow*. New York: Farrar, Straus and Giroux, 2013.

Kouzes, James M., and Barry Z. Posner. *The Leadership Challenge*, 3rd ed. San Francisco: Wiley, 2005.

Martin, Steve, Noah Goldstein, and Robert Cialdini. *The Small BIG: Small Changes That Spark Big Influence*. New York: Grand Central Publishing, 2014.

Pfeffer, Jeffrey. *Power: Why Some People Have It and Others Don't*. New York: HarperBusiness, 2010.

Pink, Daniel. (2011) *Drive: The Surprising Truth About What Motivates Us*. New York: Riverhead Books, 2011.

Pink, Daniel. (2013) *To Sell Is Human: The Surprising Truth About Moving Others*. New York: Riverhead Trade, 2013.

Thaler, Richard H., and Cass R. Sunstein. *Nudge: Improving Decisions About Health, Wealth, and Happiness*. New York: Penguin, 2009.

Vedantam, Shankar. *The Hidden Brain: How Our Unconscious Minds Elect Presidents, Control Markets, Wage Wars, and Save Our Lives*. New York: Spiegel & Geau, 2010.

Other Resources

There are many websites, podcasts, and videos (and will certainly be many more) on topics discussed in this book including influence, leadership, neuroscience, and behavioral economics. Search for the individuals listed below and you'll find useful and interesting information in a variety of formats.

- Dan Ariely
- Daniel Kahneman

- Richard Thaler
- B. J. Fogg
- Robert Cialdini
- Steve Martin (the other one)
- Simon Sinek
- Daniel Pink
- Carol Tavris
- David Rock
- Jeffrey Schwartz

BARNES & CONTI
ASSOCIATES, INC.

To succeed in the twenty-first century, you must be able to share information and move ideas into action more rapidly than ever before. Barnes & Conti Associates was established in 1985 to meet the challenging and changing needs of individuals and organizations through our public and in-house workshops, virtual classrooms, and other programs.

Barnes & Conti partners with our customers as virtual team members to achieve ongoing learning and innovation, providing flexible, just-in-time training and services that add real value and help customers achieve extraordinary business results. We focus on the complex and sophisticated leadership and interaction skills required for success in today's global organizations.

All Barnes & Conti programs can be presented in a variety of formats for intact teams or open sessions:

- Customizable, hands-on, intensive workshops
- Distance learning, including web meetings
- Learning interventions focusing on real and current work
- Site licensing for classroom or corporate intranet delivery

Some of our courses include

- Exercising Influence
- Consulting on the Inside
- The Influential Internal Consultant
- Intelligent Risk Taking
- Managing Innovation
- Creating a Culture for Risk and Innovation
- Applied Creativity

- Strategic Thinking
- Constructive Negotiation
- Constructive Debate
- Inspirational Leadership
- Art of Communication
- Leading Global and Virtual Teams
- Mastery of Change
- Facilitating Forward

At Barnes & Conti, we promise our clients and partners

- To understand your organization's mission, vision, people, processes, and issues
- To provide the highest quality programs and services, designed to support high performance and excellent business results for your organization
- To be flexible, friendly, and fast in responding to you
- To support you in applying leadership skills to real business issues in your world
- To be clear, fair, ethical, and business-like in our work with you
- To keep innovating and improving our state-of-the-art learning solutions

Please visit our website at barnesconti.com, or call 1-510-644-0911.

INDEX

Page references followed by *fig* indicate an illustrated figure; followed by *t* indicate a table.

126–127; as the reciprocal of influence, 133; shortcuts and their influence implications, 131–133. *See also* Influence

Decision making shortcuts: affect, 132; anchoring, 132; availability, 131; representativeness or familiarity, 132

Defensiveness, 89

Delegated power, 8

Describe Consequences behavior: example of community application, 31; example of work application, 29; expressive influence using, 26*fig*, 27; guidelines for choosing and when not to use, 83*t*; loss or regret aversion and use of, 129; Negotiate tactic used with, 22*t*, 83*t*

Design thinking: description of, 49; developing an influence plan using, 50–51

Difficult people, 68

Difficult situations: doing your homework on the, 77–78; handling, 68; scenarios describing various, 3–5

Direct influence behaviors: expressive influence tactics and, 21*fig*–22*t*; receptive influence tactics and, 21*fig*–22*t*

Direct power: advantages of using influence instead of, 8; benefits of leaders capability for both influence and, 9; description of, 8; limit of our, 12; limitations of using, 8; situations that require exercise of, 8

Disclose behavior: Attune tactic used with, 22*t*, 35, 36*fig*, 84*t*; community application of, 41; description of, 22*t*; guidelines for choosing and when not to use, 84*t*; home application of, 40; workplace application of, 39

Disengage tactic: influence framework on the, 21*fig*; Live to influence another day behavior of, 22*t*; as a means to an end, 119–120

Draw Out behavior: description of, 22*t*; guidelines for choosing and when not to use, 84*t*; home application of, 41; Inquire tactic used with, 35, 36*fig*, 84*t*; workplace application of, 39, 40

E-mail communication: creating opportunities for influence through, 45; influencing through, 101;

preventing problems with, 103–104; problem of failing to screen, 101; situations when it is best to avoid, 100

"Economic man" concept, 127

Electronic communication: e-mail, 45, 100–101, 103–104; getting the attention of your audience, 101–102; increasing use of, 99–100; influencing through, 100–105; preventing misunderstandings, embarrassment, and other disasters, 103–104; stimulating a productive response to, 102–103; texts, instant messaging, and beyond, 105; virtual team, 104. *See also* Social media

Emerson, Ralph Waldo, 136

Empowerment: as being open to influence of others, 12; increased opportunities for personal and business, 13

Encourage behavior: Enlist tactic used with, 22*t*, 83*t*; example of home application, 30; expressive influence by, 26*fig*, 27; guidelines for choosing and when not to use, 83*t*; how the endowment effect and, 128; representativeness or familiarity used with, 132

Endowment effect, 128

Enlist behaviors: Encourage, 22*t*, 26*fig*, 27, 30, 83*t*, 128, 132; Envision, 22*t*, 26*fig*, 27, 29, 31, 83*t*, 132; guidelines for choosing and when not to use, 83*t*

Enlist tactic: description of, 21*fig*, 22*t*; expressive influence using, 26*fig*, 27; guidelines for choosing and when not to use, 82, 83*t*

Envision behavior: applied to community, 31; applied to the workplace, 29; creating affect through use of, 132; Enlist tactic used with, 22*t*, 83*t*; expressive influence by, 26*fig*, 27; guidelines for choosing and when not to use, 83*t*. *See also* Vision

Ethics of influence: manipulation versus influence, 8, 34, 95–97, 128; negative behaviors that don't work, 98; self-interest and influence, 97–98

Expertise power, 8

misused as, 96; indirect power sometimes experienced as, 8; influence versus, 95–97; receptive influence misused as, 34, 96–97
Meetings: creating influence opportunities by setting up, 45; expressive influence used during, 29; receptive influence used in community, 41. *See also* Teams
Messages. *See* Influence message
Moral authority, 8
Mutual obligations, 8

Needs: definition of, 64; influence content influenced by, 20; reframing someone's, 65; understanding the other person's values, aspirations, and, 64–65; wants versus, 73. *See also* Express Needs behavior
Negative behaviors: ethics of using and don't work anyway, 98; manipulation, 8, 34, 95–97, 128
Negotiate behaviors: Describe Consequences, 22*t*, 26*fig*, 27, 29, 31, 83*t*, 129; guidelines for choosing and when not to use, 82, 83*t*; Offer Incentives, 22*t*, 26*fig*, 27, 29, 30, 83*t*, 130
Negotiate tactic: description of, 21*fig*, 22*t*; guidelines for choosing and when not to use, 82, 83*t*
Negotiation simulation experiment, 34
Negotiation stairstep model (BFI), 126
Neuroscience influence research, 125–126
Nonverbal behaviors: expressive influence, 27–28; receptive influence, 37. *See also* Communication
Norms, 21

Objectives. *See* Influence objectives
Observable criteria of objectives, 55, 56
Offer Incentives behavior: example of home application, 30; example of work application, 29; expressive influence using, 26*fig*, 27; guidelines for choosing and when not to use, 83*t*; reciprocity and, 130; Sell tactic used with, 22*t*, 83*t*
Offer Reasons behavior: example of community application, 30; expressive influencing using, 26*fig*,

27; guidelines for selecting, 83*t*; Tell tactic used with, 22*t*
On the fly influence, 91–92
Open-Ended Questions. *See* Ask Open-Ended Questions behavior
Open system organizations, 69–70
Opinion leaders, 122, 123
Opportunities. *See* Influence opportunities
Organizational culture: as context of influence, 21, 71; high-context versus low-context, 104; norms and taboos of, 21; values of individuals and, 21, 64–65; virtual team communication issue of, 104
Organizational factors: current issues and priorities, 20; influencing in an open system, 69–70; knowing when to exercise influence, 72; purpose and vision, 20; structure and processes, 20; understanding the power structure, 20, 70–71
Organizational learning communication, 39–40
Organizations: influence framework context component on impact of, 20; knowing when to exercise influence in, 72; open system, 69–70; understanding the power structure of your, 20, 70–71. *See also* Workplace

Paradox of failure, 135–136
Parker, Dorothy, 68
Peer relationships, 13
Persistence: in achieving influence, 57; multiple benefits of influence, 57–58
Personal power, 8
Personality: of individual impacting context of influence, 20; working with another person's interests and, 66–67
Perspective-taking research, 34
Pink, Daniel, 34
Pose Challenging Questions behavior: description of, 22*t*; Facilitate tactic used with, 22*t*, 36*fig*, 84*t*; home application of, 40; workplace application of, 38, 39
Power: direct and indirect use of, 8; information as providing confidence and, 8, 79; meaning attached to, 7; multiple sources of, 8; as potential

Santayana, George, 136
Self-confidence, 8
Self-interest: ethics of influence and, 97–98; influence content influenced by, 20; working with another person's personality, preferences, and, 66–67
Self-management: signs that you need to engage in, 90; suggestions for, 90–91
Sell behaviors: guidelines for choosing and when not to use, 83t; Offer Reasons, 26fig, 27, 30, 83t; Refer to Goals and Benefits, 22t, 26fig, 27, 29, 30, 83t, 132
Sell tactic: description of, 21fig, 22t; expressive influence using, 26fig, 27
Shaming, 98
Silence, 91
Situations: conditions for change, 78; defensiveness, resistance, and avoidance responses to, 89; doing your homework on the, 77–78; handling difficult, 68; responding to new information on the, 88; scenarios describing various difficult, 3–5; when to avoid e-mail communication, 100. *See also* Current issues
Skills as power, 8
Sloan School of Management at MIT, 78
Social media: economic man concept and influencers of the, 127; providing a new method for influencing groups, 107–108; writing and posting an influential post or article, 109–110. *See also* Electronic communication
Social proof, 129
Sphere of influence: description of, 9; diagram for charting your current, 10fig; examples of your, 10–11; external factors which may impact your, 12; social media used to expand your, 107–110
Sphere of influence examples: of direct influence, 11; of indirect influence, 11, 117–120; typical and common, 10
Stairstep model of negotiation (FBI), 126
Stories/storytelling, 132
Strengths versus limitations, 74
Structure (organizational), 20

Suggest behavior: expressive influence using, 26; guidelines for choosing and when not to use, 83t; Tell tactic used with, 22t, 26fig, 83t
Supportive criteria of objectives, 55, 57

Taboos, 21
Tactics: cultural behaviors versus, 71; debate used as indirect influence, 119; disengage, 21fig, 22t, 119–120; expressive influence behaviors and, 21fig–22t, 26fig–31, 83t, 96; receptive influence behaviors and, 22t–23, 35–36fig, 38–42, 84t, 96–97
Teams: actively engage in influence, 123–124; do your homework on the, 122–123; electronic communication issues for virtual, 104; establish a climate for influence, 122; expanding your influence impact on the, 121; knowing when to exercise influence, 72; understanding the power relationships in the, 20. *See also* Meetings; Workplace
Tell behaviors: Express Needs, 22t, 26fig, 83t; guidelines for choosing and when not to use, 83t; influence objectives by using the, 55; Suggest, 22t, 26fig, 83t. *See also* Communication
Tell tactic: communicating influence objectives using behaviors of, 55; considerations for selecting, 82, 83t; description of, 21fig, 22t
Test Implications behaviors: description of, 22t; guidelines for choosing and when not to use, 84t; home applications of, 40, 41; Listen tactic used with, 35, 36fig, 84t; workplace application of, 39
Texts communication, 105
Thai high-context culture, 104
Thaler, Richard, 128
"Theater game," 75
Threats: defensiveness, resistance, and avoidance responses to feeling, 89; fight or flight response to, 126; manipulation through, 96; as negative behavior that doesn't work, 98
"Tip the balance," 118
Tit-for-tat, 98
To Sell Is Human (Pink), 34